Secrets to Winning
at Office Politics

Secrets to Winning
at Office Politics

How to
Achieve Your
Goals and Increase
Your Influence
at Work

Marie G. McIntyre, Ph.D.

 St. Martin's Griffin ✠ New York

www.stmartins.com

Design by Patrice Sheridan

LIBRARY OF CONGRESS CATALOGING-IN-PUBLICATION DATA

McIntyre, Marie G., 1947–
  Secrets to winning at office politics: how to achieve your goals and increase your influence at work / Marie McIntyre.
      p. cm.
  Includes bibliographical references (page 257).
  ISBN 0-312-33218-1
  EAN 978-0-312-33218-1
  1. Office Politics.   2. Interpersonal relations.   I. Title.

HF5386.5M38 2005
650.1'3—dc22   2005042779

First Edition: July 2005

10 9 8 7 6 5 4 3 2 1

To my husband, John,
for the priceless gifts of love, encouragement,
friendship, and laughter

Contents

Part III How to Become a Winner   157

Acknowledgments

Turning an idea into a published book is definitely a team effort. Without the guidance and assistance of my agent, Farley Chase, this particular book would never have become a reality. Farley saw the value in the concept and encouraged me to consider a wider audience for the book. He made helpful suggestions about the initial chapters, provided invaluable assistance in crafting the book proposal, and, most important, sold the book to a terrific publisher. He is also an absolute pleasure to work with. Farley, there's no way that I can thank you enough! I have also been fortunate to collaborate with two talented editors at St. Martin's Press: Marian Lizzi, who made very useful suggestions about the book's structure, and Sheila Curry Oakes, whose contributions definitely improved the final manuscript. Julie Mente helped to shepherd the book through each stage of the publication process. Iris Bass and Shea Kornblum also made valuable contributions.

My husband, John Gambs, who is always encouraging and supportive, definitely went above and beyond the call of spousal duty with this book. As I was writing, he read every chapter at least twice, providing helpful feedback, then read the entire book again before it was submitted to the publisher. Gail Rogers, a life-long friend who also runs a large organization, reviewed an early draft and suggested useful changes. Thanks also to JoAnn Pinder, Katherine Sherrington, and Sally Sherrington, who graciously consented to read and comment on the final version. Jennifer Padgett and Julie Dobrinska who work in my consulting business, also provided assistance. Jennifer created the attractive and professional proposal packages that were submitted to publishers, and Julie was the final reader of the manuscript. Thanks, J & J, both for your help with the book and for keeping me sane on a daily basis.

The mentors and managers who provided guidance, advice, and opportunities earlier in my career helped to lay the foundation for the perspectives offered in this book. I particularly want to express my appreciation to Dr. Stan Smits, who has been both a mentor and a friend for many years. Stan, my life would have been quite different without your influence. Thanks also to Bill Anderson, my first role model for management; Page Truitt, who took a risk in making me the first female manager in our organization; Jim Stephens, who introduced me to leadership development; the late Jay Levergood, who provided my introduction to the inner workings of the corporate executive suite; and Ginny Hall, my role model for self-employment.

I also want to express great gratitude to my clients. You are the reason that I find my work rewarding, and I have learned a lot from our work together. Many of the insights offered in this book developed from the problems, frustrations, successes, and strategies that you have shared with me over the years. I believe that readers will benefit greatly from your experiences.

Finally, deep love and appreciation to the rest of my family members: My brother, Michael McIntyre, who is also one of my closest friends. My daughter, Katherine Hoover, who has been a source of joy since the day she was born and is now a truly amazing adult. Her husband, Steve Hoover, who seems more like a son than a son-in-law and is just about the best dad I have ever seen. And Marie Allison, Alex, Camille, and Zachary, who enrich my life more than they will ever know. I am also eternally grateful to my late parents, Bill and Katherine McIntyre, who gave their children the gifts of love, trust, self-confidence, and a strong set of values. They were my first and most important role models, and are still a source of inspiration. When it comes to family, I am a most fortunate person.

Preface

Several years ago, another consultant and I invited a mutual client, a man whom we shall call Todd, out to lunch. Our hope was that we could keep him from destroying his career. Todd was an extremely bright, capable executive with a clear and inspired vision for his organization. He had a true passion for his work and a great desire to do good things in the world. The problem, however, was that he had gotten completely sidetracked by his intense animosity toward his boss, embarking on an obsessive quest to get this man fired. As outside observers, my colleague and I could readily see that, if this war continued, the inevitable outcome would be Todd's own termination. Todd, however, could not see this at all. So, as we ate our sandwiches, the two of us tried to help Todd view the situation more clearly. No luck. Todd spent the entire lunch ranting about his boss's failings and the general unfairness of his circumstances. As we predicted, Todd was soon looking for another job. Many people experience difficulties at work because they do not accurately "read" their environment or correctly anticipate the consequences of their actions. Unlike Todd, however, most of them are able to correct the situation once they understand the problem. That is why I decided to write this book.

Work is truly a critical component of happiness. Unlike the other creatures on the planet, people need to have a purpose. Those whose lives lack meaning feel lost and often drift into harmful, self-destructive activities. Meaningful work may be paid or unpaid, inside or outside the home—but for many of us, our sense of purpose is connected to our jobs. Unfortunately, if people lack clear goals, have unpleasant working relationships, or simply don't understand how organizations operate, the joy of accomplishment is often replaced by frustration and disappointment. When people fail to master the political side of work, their jobs may become unrewarding and unhealthy.

DISCOVERING MY OWN PURPOSE

Some people find their purpose in life quite early. From the time he was twelve, my high school boyfriend was operating a radio transmitter in his house, from which he broadcast to the neighborhood. He now owns a radio station. Others find a new mission later in life. My multitalented husband discovered a gift and passion for songwriting in his forties. And some of us have a purpose that we may not immediately recognize. Although I always felt my jobs were meaningful, I didn't see the pattern in my own work until I had been employed for many years.

Earlier in my career, I occupied a variety of roles: helping people with disabilities find employment, resolving disputes between employees and managers, counseling people who had lost their jobs, teaching managers to be more effective leaders, encouraging communication between executives and the workforce. I spent more time in institutions of higher learning than any sane person probably should, acquiring degrees in psychology, counseling, and management. During those years, I was a counselor, trainer, manager, and human resources director. I worked in business, government, and not-for-profit organizations. For a long time, I viewed these experiences as simply a collection of different jobs, the natural result of my desire to always be learning and doing new things.

When I decided to return to graduate school to get a Ph.D., I spent some time exploring what I really wanted to do. That was when I realized that the common theme throughout my career has been the connection between people and work. My own purpose, I believe, is to help others find greater rewards in their work and overcome any obstacles that are getting in the way—including their own behavior. During my exploration of various graduate programs, one professor posed an interesting question. "If you could accomplish anything with your life, what would it be?" he asked. Reflecting back on my career to that point, I replied, "Actually, I wish that I could help people understand how organizations operate and help organizations understand how people operate." It seemed like an unrealistic aspiration at the time, but now that's exactly what I do.

THE PREVALENCE OF POLITICS

Since leaving the employ of others, I have operated my own consulting business, working with a wide variety of organizations. My clients have included companies in telecommunications, retail, food processing, insurance, advertising, accounting, pharmaceuticals, consulting, software, manufacturing, transaction processing, and health care. I have also worked with many government agencies (local, state, and federal) and not-for-profit organizations.

Despite the diversity of settings in which I work, the same issues arise with remarkable consistency. Here are a few of the people that I encounter on a regular basis:

- A confused and anxious employee who is not sure exactly what is expected by management

- A tired and angry person who is clearly in the wrong job
- A frustrated manager who does not know how to deal with a poorly performing employee
- People at all levels who feel that their boss is incompetent, unfair, or unreasonable
- Colleagues who have constant disagreements because of drastically different work styles
- Entire departments at war with each other because of conflicting roles
- Many, many people who feel that they are somehow being treated unfairly

All these unhappy folks are, in one way or another, dealing with political dilemmas. When you view "office politics" not as a Machiavellian plot, but as a normal aspect of work that needs to be managed, you quickly realize that political ability is a fundamental component of success in any job. Political topics are seldom discussed openly, however. At work, it is usually not appropriate to mention that you are furious with your boss, angling for a promotion, afraid of a colleague, or worried about your future. So people suffer in silence, feeling helpless to deal with their political predicaments and growing increasingly frustrated.

THE NEED FOR POLITICAL MENTORING

Through my consulting work, I have helped many employees, managers, and executives figure out how to handle their personal political challenges. My clients are not screwups or troublemakers, but competent and successful people wrestling with stressful issues that are difficult to resolve. Simply talking about these problems is often a great relief for them. In our confidential conversations, they can freely express their frustration with dysfunctional bosses, career uncertainties, challenging staff members, derailed projects, or obstructive colleagues. Listening to their difficulties, I have come to fully appreciate how much our mental and physical well-being is affected by what happens on the job.

For some, the answer to their political dilemma is as simple as shifting their expectations, taking time to consider a different point of view, or having a focused discussion with a colleague. For others, the solution may require some serious self-examination and a change in long-standing behavior patterns. In either case, a political mentor can serve as a sounding board and offer a different perspective on the situation. This is frequently my role with clients. In writing this book, my goal is to provide the same assistance for readers: to help them view their circumstances differently, keep them from becoming their own worst enemy, and suggest some new strategies and approaches.

Each section of the book deals with a different aspect of workplace politics. The first section, Mastering the Fundamentals, describes basic realities of organizational life and the essential components of Political Intelligence. The second, Avoiding Political Pitfalls, discusses the destructive games and personal blunders that can lead an unsuspecting individual into a political quagmire. Finally, How to Become a Winner provides specific strategies that can improve your political position and increase your influence. My hope is that this book will help you achieve your own personal and business goals, whatever they may be, so that work can become an even more enjoyable and meaningful part of your life.

A note to colleagues and clients: This book contains many examples. Although all are true stories, the names, titles, and/or occupations have been changed. If you believe you recognize yourself (or someone else), please keep in mind that many people have similar problems, dilemmas, and challenges. You may very well see yourself in someone else's story. Examples are useful because people learn much more from reality than they do from abstract concepts. The life experiences of my clients and colleagues have made an invaluable contribution to this book, to its readers, and to my own political education. For that, I am deeply appreciative.

A Note to Readers: If you would like to share your own political stories, dilemmas, or insights, please visit my Web site at www.mariemcintyre.com. I'd love to hear from you!

Part I

MASTERING THE

FUNDAMENTALS

Chapter 1

Politics Is Not a Dirty Word

Playing politics is like having sex. Almost everybody does it, but nobody is comfortable discussing exactly what they do. We will talk for hours, however, about what other people might be doing. Typically, we use the term "playing politics" only to describe our colleagues' behavior—never our own. *They* are sucking up, scheming, and manipulating, but *we* are building relationships, developing strategies, and opening communication channels.

Many people feel that playing the political game involves devious plotting or blatant self-promotion. But in reality, "politics" is what naturally happens whenever people with different goals, interests, and personalities try to work together. We are all continuously engaged in political transactions throughout the normal course of every workday. The process itself is neither good nor bad, but simply a fact of life—and the morality of the outcome is determined entirely by the motives and goals of the players. Both Hitler and Mother Teresa might be considered "politically adept," but their results are judged rather differently.

HOW DO YOU WIN AT POLITICS?

The political side of work quickly becomes apparent as soon as we take our first job. To succeed, we not only have to do outstanding work, but we also have to deal with quirky bosses and annoying co-workers. Colleagues get defensive when we point out their mistakes, unscrupulous rivals try to stab us in the back, and managers make decisions that seem totally unfair—or completely idiotic. Learning to deal with these realities, and succeed in spite of them, constitutes our on-the-job political education. Every office is a playing field for the game of politics. And when you take a job, you're automatically a player.

Kelly learned this lesson the hard way. After graduating from college with a marketing degree, she accepted an administrative assistant position in the marketing department of a large corporation, viewing it as a temporary step toward her professional career. But as the months passed, Kelly became increasingly discouraged. Every time she applied for a promotion, she was rejected, with no clear explanation of the reason. Finally, feeling trapped and desperate, she went to her boss and asked for some honest feedback. Much to her surprise, Kelly learned that people viewed her as egotistical and arrogant—the unanticipated result of her desire to get into a marketing position. Striving to be noticed by management, Kelly had tried to demonstrate her superior knowledge and skills at every opportunity, but this tactic had backfired. Her condescending manner completely alienated the other assistants, who quickly spread the word that she was difficult to work with, thereby killing her chances of being promoted. Kelly was stunned by the feedback—but her political education had begun. In her eagerness to succeed, Kelly made a common mistake: she failed to realize that managing the political environment is just as important as managing tasks and responsibilities.

Winning this game means acquiring the political power necessary to accomplish the goals that matter to you. We sometimes equate success only with rapid advancement, but not everyone is interested in promotions. Autonomy, security, responsibility, skill development, challenge, and interesting work are a few of the other rewards that people often hope to find through their jobs. When I recently surveyed 220 people from business and government organizations about their views on office politics, these were some of the responses to the question, "When people are good at politics, what are they able to do?"

- Get their projects moved up the priority list
- Play golf with important people
- Influence management
- Have their own office
- Bypass normal procedures
- Advance quickly
- Get asked to solve the toughest problems
- Receive more recognition
- Accomplish results
- Get things done despite great obstacles
- Get senior management to "buy in" on projects
- Help bring about changes
- Get other people to do their work
- Draw attention to a project
- Get more money in their budget
- Acquire resources for their staff
- Stay out of trouble
- Have their ideas heard
- Get raises when other people don't
- Survive changes

The common theme running through these answers is that politics is about getting what you want, whatever that may be. And to get what you want, you must be able to influence others. Kelly provides a clear example of political failure: she has inadvertently created adversarial relationships that present a serious obstacle to reaching her career goals. To respond to this catastrophe, she needs a political strategy that will reverse the negative opinions held by her co-workers and her boss. If she succeeds in shifting these perceptions, her odds of moving into a marketing slot will greatly increase.

Although a well-crafted political game plan can represent the difference between success and failure, candid discussion of strategic maneuvers sometimes makes people uneasy. Purposeful strategizing is often mistakenly viewed as scheming or plotting. In Kelly's situation, a wise mentor might suggest that she needs to cease her obvious self-promotion and seek out opportunities to assist her colleagues. There is nothing manipulative about this advice—it's just practical . . . and beneficial for the business as well. Increased cooperation among the assistants should not only improve Kelly's image, but also help the department run more smoothly. Although she needs to be less blatant about it, Kelly should continue to look for chances to get to know managers in the marketing department and to demonstrate her potential. You always have a better shot at accomplishing your goals if the people in power support you, but they can hardly support you if they don't know who you are. Making yourself known in appropriate ways is simply smart—but talking about specific tactics can make people cringe a bit.

Just as some have a natural aptitude for math, music, or golf, others seem to possess innate political talent. These instinctive abilities give them the same competitive advantage at work that natural athletes have in sports. But while you can improve your golf score by signing up for lessons, it's pretty tough to find tutoring in office politics. Because the frank discussion of strategy is frowned upon, people with political dilemmas often have to suffer in silence. By openly discussing the "secrets" of office politics and describing the attitudes, behaviors, and approaches that contribute to success, this book is designed to help you understand and manage the political process in your organization. So here's lesson number one: to win at office politics, you must first clearly define your goals.

WHAT DO YOU WANT?

If you took a poll and asked people why they work, what do you think they would say? Money is usually the first reason that comes to mind, but in addition to financial security, work provides many other benefits: we can learn new skills, interact with congenial people, take pride in accomplishments, and identify with a meaningful purpose. Although we complain about our jobs and dream about vacations, most of us get a lot more from work than just a paycheck.

Let's consider two people who represent opposite extremes in their political goals. First we have Sergio, a young sales manager who knows exactly how he wants his entire career to unfold. Sergio likes the company he works for and hopes to stay there. He has a plan: first, transfer to a position with a larger sales territory, then apply for a regional director job, with the ultimate goal of becoming vice president for North American sales—and CEO wouldn't be out of the question. Sergio is clearly an ambitious, goal-driven guy.

At the other extreme, we find Joan, an executive assistant in the legal department of a large corporation. "I really don't have any work goals," she said to me. "I just come in every day and do my job." This sounded like someone working mostly for a paycheck, so I inquired about her life outside of work. Her whole face lit up as she enthusiastically described her community and church activities. Like many people, Joan is motivated by something other than her job and works primarily to finance the rest of her life. But she actually does have goals related to work: she wants to remain employed and enjoy her time at the office as much as possible. People whose eyes glaze over when asked about their goals often find it much easier to answer this question: "How would you like things to be different?" Joan had a ready answer for that one. She was getting a little bored and wished that her work could be more interesting. Politically speaking, Sergio needs to position himself for the next promotion, while Joan needs to acquire some new responsibilities or find a more rewarding position.

As an organizational psychologist, I frequently encounter people who are having difficulty with some aspect of their job. They may be uncertain of their next career move, angry at a demanding boss, excluded from an important project, annoyed with uncooperative colleagues, afraid of failing at a tough new assignment, unsure of how to sell an idea to management, burned out from ongoing job stress, or experiencing a host of other problems. After we discuss their dilemma, my first question is always the same: "What are your personal goals in this situation?" If they aren't sure of the answer, then that's where we start, because all subsequent decisions and actions need to be driven by their own individual desires.

An old saying provides this advice: "If you're not sure where you're going, you'll probably end up somewhere else." When thinking about your goals, here are some questions to consider:

- Do you want to stay with your current organization or find a different place to work?
- Do you want to remain in the same field or consider a different occupation?
- Would you like a more comfortable relationship with your boss?
- Do you want to be given more challenging and interesting assignments?
- Are you interested in getting promoted or expanding your responsibilities?
- Do you want more recognition for your contributions or accomplishments?
- Would you like a better working relationship with certain people or departments?
- Do you simply want to keep your current job in order to finance the rest of your life?

Sharpening your political ability can increase the odds of accomplishing whatever objectives are important to you, but first you must clearly differentiate between goals and wishes.

THE DIFFERENCE BETWEEN
A GOAL AND A WISH

When we are having problems at work, we often think in terms of wishes, not goals.

"I wish that I could make more money."
"I wish I had gotten that promotion instead of Susan."
"I wish that my boss wasn't such a moron."
"I wish my employees would pay attention to deadlines."
"I wish a headhunter would call and offer me a job."

Wishing is a passive activity that can easily degenerate into whining and complaining. Goals, on the other hand, help to define the actions we need to take. The more time we spend wishing, the less time we spend actually accomplishing anything. Fortunately, our wishes usually contain clues to our political objectives.

The CEO of a health-care company hired me to provide some coaching for Jeff, an executive who was driving him crazy. After a reorganization, Jeff no longer reported to the CEO, but to a newly hired senior vice president, yet Jeff was acting as though this change had never happened, continuing to go to the CEO for information and seldom responding to requests from his new boss. He frequently made snide, sarcastic remarks about the situation within earshot of the CEO. "Do something about him," the CEO ordered. "He's got a lot of future potential here, but not if he keeps acting like this!" When Jeff and I got together, he embarked on a long, rambling tirade about unqualified executives, stupid decisions, and general unfairness. Then I asked the key questions: "What do you want in this situation, Jeff? What are your goals? Are you planning on a career with this company or are you ready to leave?"

Without the answer to these questions, Jeff's future course of action is unclear. If he is so disillusioned that he wants to seek greener pastures elsewhere, then he needs to begin making outside contacts. On the other hand, if he plans to remain with this company, he needs to be perceived as a helpful, contributing member of the management team. When we first met, however, he was expending his energy in the least productive way possible: obsessing about the past, complaining about his new boss, and wishing that things would magically return to their previous state.

Jeff responded that he did indeed want to stay with his company, but wished that he could return to his previous level. If that is his goal, he has additional questions to consider: "What can you do to move in that direction? And is your current behavior helping?" Clearly it wasn't, but Jeff hadn't previously thought about it that way—in fact, he really wasn't thinking at all. He was angry and hurt and acting out his feelings. Once he decided to stop focusing on his resentment, he could consider the future and define his goals. Having chosen to stay with his company, Jeff now had a clear guideline to follow when interacting with others (including his new boss): What would a cooperative and committed member of the management team do in this situation? By using this guideline to make conscious decisions about his behavior, he was able to repair his management relationships and get back on a positive career track.

Wishes put the focus on what we want "them" to do. Goals highlight what we can do ourselves. Wishes take us out of the power position by implying that we are at the mercy of others. Goals give us power by describing results that we intend to accomplish. When converted to goals, the wishes on page 9 would look like this:

"I am going to develop the skills I need for a higher-paying job."
"I will ask my manager about how to prepare myself for the next available promotion."
"I am going to start communicating in a more positive way with my boss."
"I am going to discuss the importance of deadlines with my employees and see that they meet them."
"I plan to update my résumé and start checking out jobs in my field."

Goals imply action. Wishes imply sitting around and waiting for something to happen. Changing from wishful thinking to goal-directed planning doesn't guarantee that you will get what you want, but it certainly increases your odds.

FOUR POLITICAL TYPES

Typically, our goals at work fall into two categories: business and personal. Business goals relate to the responsibilities of your position, such as accomplishing expected results, developing creative approaches to problems, and doing anything else that will make the organization more successful. Personal goals, on the other hand, focus on what you want for yourself, such as developing new abilities, getting assigned to interesting projects, or being promoted to a higher position. Sometimes our actions help us to achieve these goals, and sometimes they have the opposite effect. Jeff's childish response to getting a new boss, for example, was clearly harmful to both his career and his company.

Four common political types can be described by the way their behavior affects both business and personal goals, as shown in the table below. See if any of these people sound familiar to you.

	Behavior **Helps** *Personal Goals*	Behavior **Hurts** *Personal Goals*
Behavior **Helps** *Business Goals*	Winner	Martyr
Behavior **Hurts** *Business Goals*	Sociopath	Dimwit

Martyrs try to help their organizations, but at high personal cost to themselves. They usually wind up feeling unappreciated and resentful, an attitude that eventually bleeds over into their interactions with others, no matter how they may try to hide it. And some of them don't try to hide it at all. Eventually Martyrs burn out, either personally or professionally.

Emily, a vice president of customer service, provides a prime example of a self-sacrificing Martyr: For many years, she reported to a relentlessly demanding CEO, who constantly changed Emily's goals, bombarded her with requests for information, repeatedly criticized her staff, and denied all her requests for additional resources. Periodically, he would also tell her how important she was to him, confide in her about confidential problems, and insist that she was the only person he could really trust. Despite her growing fatigue and depression, Emily continued to try to do everything the CEO expected, working longer and longer hours and becoming increasingly stressed by his ever-changing demands. Imagine her shock and dismay when she learned through the grapevine that the CEO was interviewing candidates for her job! Ironically, the CEO had come to view obliging and obedient Emily as an unassertive doormat. Her eventual replacement worked fewer hours, was allowed to hire more staff, and was paid twice as much.

Emily was a pathological pleaser, but Martyrs also come in a more militant variety—crusaders who are true believers in a cause. Although crusading Martyrs usually have the interests of the organization at heart, their approach to advocacy often torpedoes their own career. When these Martyrs jump on their soapbox, their adamant and single-minded preaching tends to make people run the other way; for example: the dedicated quality assurance specialist whose finger-pointing about defective products alienates her manufacturing colleagues; the brilliant corporate attorney whom managers try to circumvent because he always throws up roadblocks to their plans; the social worker who rants about bureaucratic barriers so frequently that no one hears her valid complaints about policies that are harmful to clients. Ironically, their poorly handled quest to make things better usually deprives these Martyrs of the very influence they seek.

Sociopaths are interested only in their own needs, wants, and desires. Their self-centered fixation on personal goals damages their organizations—but they don't care about that. This comment from the survey on about office politics provides an apt description of Sociopaths: "Able to achieve a certain amount of success, but their actions tend to come back to haunt them in one way or another." Sociopathic executives can wreak havoc on a company, as illustrated by the corporate scandals involving CEOs who appropriate company funds for lavish personal indulgences or who use illegal accounting procedures to enrich themselves at the expense of employees and shareholders. Other executive Sociopaths have been known to award themselves large bonuses while their companies were losing money and employees were losing jobs. But selfishness is not the exclusive property of top management—many Sociopaths can be found at lower levels as well. This unsavory group includes not only people who steal time, money, equipment, or customers, but also those who meet personal objectives in a way that creates problems for others. Jeremy was a compensation specialist who did virtually no work. He sat in his office all day, reading magazines, making personal calls, and doing crossword puzzles. Every so often he would crank out a report or a memo to keep up appearances. Jeremy was essentially stealing from his company by accepting a paycheck for work he never performed. Because he had once won a discrimination lawsuit, he thought that no one would have the nerve to fire him. For several years, he was right.

A different variety of Sociopath is exemplified by Victoria, a computer technician. For many years, Victoria was engaged in a long-term affair with the married head of her department, who was several levels above her in the organization. Because she made her "special connections" widely known, she became a political untouchable and used this status to intimidate anyone who got in her way. If something displeased her, she would blast co-workers with scathing e-mails that were always copied to her boyfriend. She demanded to be included in highly technical projects although she lacked the necessary skills. People throughout the company tried to steer clear of any endeavor that involved Victoria because she was so difficult to work with. Her immediate supervisor felt completely powerless, because he knew that any conversation with Victoria about performance issues would immediately result in unwelcome attention from the department head (who obviously shared the blame for this disastrous situation).

Because they often do succeed in obtaining immediate personal benefits, in the short run Sociopaths can look like political winners. However, their self-centeredness almost always limits their long-term success. Because of her difficult reputation, Victoria remained stuck in a dead-end job (and probably a dead-end affair as well). Jeremy was eventually let go. And many sociopathic executives have lost their jobs, forced their companies into bankruptcy, or gone to jail.

Dimwits exhibit behavior that is both self-destructive and harmful to the organization. Their actions seem to be driven by psychological needs over which they have little control. Mark was a chronically angry Dimwit. In meetings, he verbally attacked co-workers who disagreed with him, storming out of the room if he seemed to be losing the argument. He raised vehement objections to any new idea, especially those that might create extra work for him. He felt no hesitation about yelling at his boss (always a dangerous practice). Eventually, he was fired. Don, a lustful Dimwit, was a partner in a small business. Whenever an attractive woman joined the staff, he would flirt with her, put his arm around her, and ask "joking" questions about her sex life. When the company became involved in a sexual harassment lawsuit, Don was personally embarrassed, and the business suffered as well. Lucinda, a management Dimwit, believed that the way to improve her staff's performance was to berate them for mistakes on a regular basis.

Even when she tried to be positive, her negative impulses eventually took over. After giving a motivational speech about all the good work the group had done that year and all the exciting things they could do in the future, she ended by saying, "And if you don't like it here, you can just leave!" Many of them did. Lucinda's staff turnover rate increased every year, eventually causing top management to investigate the situation. Lucinda herself was "turned over" shortly thereafter.

Winners are people whose behavior at work contributes to both business and personal success. I believe that these are the folks who succeed at office politics, especially in the long run. Glenn was a Winner. He joined his company as an accountant, but knew that he wanted to do more. As his career progressed, he learned about other areas of finance, took on several highly visible projects, delivered results in the face of difficult obstacles, got to know company executives, and developed many positive working relationships. Glenn became known as a pleasant, helpful person who always did an outstanding job. Eventually, he moved through several management positions to become vice president of finance for the largest division in his company. At each step, he tried to improve operations and help his staff develop new skills and abilities. Some people may have envied Glenn's success, but almost everyone agreed that it was well-deserved.

Those who consistently behave like Martyrs, Sociopaths, or Dimwits are doomed to eventual failure and disappointment. Their political power is automatically limited by their excessive behavior, which gradually alienates everyone around them. Although most of us are not so extreme, we all act out of bitterness, selfishness, or uncontrolled emotion from time to time. Sadly, these destructive tendencies prevent many people from reaching their full potential as Winners.

One goal of this book is to help you spot your own political weaknesses and take steps to correct them. There are no perfect people. We all have little deviations in our personalities that make us unique, interesting, and sometimes annoying—and what a boring world it would be otherwise! So keep your endearing eccentricities—but consider changing any behaviors that may reduce your influence, harm your working relationships, or keep you from getting what you want. Remember, you may have the intentions of a Winner, but your actions will determine how you are viewed by others.

THE ETHICS OF OFFICE POLITICS

Ruthless and immoral players give the game of office politics a bad name. Fortunately, however, the ethically impaired almost always experience an eventual downfall. Because people driven solely by personal gain or other selfish motives are seldom successful in the long run, winning the political game requires that you consider the ethical implications of your decisions. Given that most of us work for pay, ethical issues on the job often come down to the question of what we are willing to do for money. Only a tiny minority of people would agree to kill or harm someone for cash. But, would you lie? Falsify records? Fail to report violations of law? Tolerate unsafe working conditions? Your automatic response is likely to be, "No, of course not!" Think about it another way, though: imagine you'll be fired if you refuse to falsify a report. Now, would you do it?

In the realm of ethics, only actions count. Your moral code is communicated not by what you say you believe, but by what your behavior actually demonstrates. During the course of a career, almost everyone will encounter **Ethical Moments**—situations that force us to decide whether or not to live up to our personal standards. One of my Ethical Moments occurred when I was responsible for internal communications in a large corporation. When a high-level manager suggested sending out false information to employees, I realized that lying to people who relied on me for accuracy was not something I could live with. But I did not leap to my feet and cry, "You liar! How could you ask me to do such a thing?" Instead, I simply explained that if we were caught in an obvious lie, our future credibility would be ruined. Fortunately, this pragmatic reasoning was accepted by the executive, whose value system did not exactly highlight honesty. I was relieved not to have to lay my career on the line for this issue, but I did realize that I would resign before sending out information that was blatantly untrue. Such decisions are easier when you have clearly defined your moral parameters.

This Political Golden Rule should be followed by anyone hoping to become a Winner:

**Never advance your own interests by
harming the business or hurting other people.**

If you feel this is overly altruistic, then consider some practical realities. Selfish and mean-spirited actions will likely provoke similar responses from others in the future. Assistance may not be forthcoming when you need it, and nasty rumors about you may spring up on the office grapevine. If you help yourself in ways that hurt the business—by lying, stealing, taking unacceptable shortcuts, or doing substandard work—you run the risk of getting caught and seriously damaging your career. So, whether you are motivated by moral or practical considerations, following the Political Golden Rule is more likely to promote your long-term political and professional success.

Personal Politics

The Personal Politics section at the end of each chapter is intended to help you relate the "secrets" of winning at office politics to your own work situation. By the end of the book, you will be able to create a detailed Political Game Plan for accomplishing your goals. But the first step is to convert your wishes into goal statements.

Are You Focused on Wishes or Goals?

Assessing your situation:

- Create a mental picture of your working life as you would like for it to be two years into the future. Close your eyes, if that helps. Or draw a picture, if that works for you. Once you have a clear image of the ideal future in mind, list everything that would be different from the way it is now. These are your wishes.

Moving from assessment to action:

- To actually create your ideal future, you need to convert your wishes into goal statements, because goals force you to focus on what you yourself could do to change the situation. Don't waste your energy thinking about what someone else should be doing—that won't get you anywhere. Look at your wish list and convert those wishes into goals. If you're not sure how to do that, the steps are described below, then summarized in a table.

1. **Define the specific result that you hope to achieve.** For example, saying, "I want more money" isn't specific enough. You could accomplish that by robbing a bank or

murdering your wealthy aunt. But saying, "I want a job that pays twice what I'm making now" is pretty clear.

2. **Consider what obstacles are keeping you from that result.** In the example of the higher-paying job, obstacles might include a lack of education, a limited career path, or being perceived negatively by the people who make promotional decisions.

3. **Now here's the hard part. Figure out what you personally can do to overcome those obstacles.** For example, if you lack education, how can you get it? Or, if you're in a job with limited potential, what can you do to get into a more promising field? If certain people perceive you negatively, how can you begin to change those perceptions?

4. **Turn those ideas into goal statements.** A goal statement starts with "I," uses an action verb, and describes something specific that you will do; such as, "I will get information about degree programs with class schedules that fit my work hours," or "I will research career options that fit my skills and experience," or "I will talk with my boss about how to get considered for a promotion."

5. **For each goal, identify the first step toward accomplishing it. Then do it. Then take the next one.** Big goals often seem much more manageable if you simply focus on the next specific action that you need to take.

Turning Wishes into Goals

1. **Desired Result:** What do I specifically want?

   _____

2. **Obstacles:** What is keeping me from getting what I want?

   _____

3. **Personal Actions:** What can I personally do to overcome those obstacles?

   _____

4. **Goal Statement:** "I will . . ."

   _____

5. **The First Step:** What specific step do I need to take *now*?

   _____

What Is Your Political Type?

Assessing your situation:

- If you have recognized yourself as a Martyr, Sociopath, or Dimwit, you need to change some fundamental attitudes about your work situation. What basic beliefs are getting you in trouble? Do you feel that you need to please everyone? Be in control of every situation? Always be right? Get your own way? List the attitudes that may be causing you problems. Then list the unproductive behaviors generated by those attitudes.
- Even if you are a Winner, you may occasionally lapse into harmful behaviors. Do you ever find yourself acting like a Martyr, Sociopath, or Dimwit? If so, what specifically are you doing? What would an outside observer see? List any behaviors that might keep you from achieving your work or career goals.

Moving from assessment to action:

- Now that you have identified your unproductive behaviors, determine what you will do differently in the future. Beside each negative behavior, list the positive behavior that will replace it. For example, if you have listed, "I respond angrily when colleagues won't do what I want," then the replacement behavior might be, "When colleagues won't do what I want, I will ask questions to understand their point of view and try to reach a compromise." Specific suggestions on changing behavior are provided at the end of chapter 6.

What Are Your Ethical Dilemmas?

Assessing your situation:

- Does your job present any potential ethical challenges? Do you admire the ethical standards of management in your organization? Are you ever asked to do things that don't feel quite right?

Moving from assessment to action:

- If you have ethical conflicts at work, you have three choices: (1) continue to compromise your own standards because of the other benefits provided by your job; (2) try to change the situation by discussing it with the appropriate people; or (3) find a more compatible place to work. Only you can decide which is the best course in your situation.

Chapter 2

Political Intelligence
and the Facts of Life

To be a Winner at office politics, you must accept certain fundamental truths about the way organizations operate. Unfortunately, these realities often conflict with cherished beliefs held by those of us raised in a democratic society. To illustrate the problems created by unrealistic expectations, let's consider the sad story of Alan. Although he undoubtedly would describe himself as a victim of politics, Alan actually committed workplace suicide though a complete lack of political ability.

Political Warfare:
The True Story of Alan and Barbara

Alan was extremely excited about his new job as executive director of the Horizon Center, a large counseling agency located in a metropolitan area. In his previous position, Alan had found himself embroiled in numerous conflicts with his boss, who was a fool, and several staff members, who were borderline incompetent and had no interpersonal skills. At least, that was Alan's opinion. But now, those problems were in the past.

On his first day, Alan met with the staff to describe his vision for the Horizon Center. He wanted to upgrade facilities, expand services, and increase the center's influence in the community. He felt that the center should go beyond helping individuals and become more involved in public education about mental health issues. The staff was energized—they couldn't wait to start moving in this new direction. A few days later, Alan made the same speech to his board of directors, but was disappointed by their lukewarm response. The chairperson, Barbara, kept having side conversations during his presentation and even left the room to check on arrangements for lunch. The remainder of the board meeting involved operational decisions Alan felt should have been left up to him. He concluded that these people didn't really understand how a board was supposed to function.

During the next few weeks, Alan began to implement changes with the enthusiastic support of his staff. But several meetings with Barbara convinced him that she was completely clueless about the proper role of a board chair. Although he tried to teach her about management and help her understand his plan, she only seemed interested in expense report procedures, client record-keeping, and the redecoration of the lobby. Unfortunately, since Barbara had just been elected to a two-year term, he was stuck with her. As he learned more about her background, Alan decided that Barbara was only on the board because her family had money and was related to the mayor. Growing up in a poor family, Alan had watched rich, connected people in his hometown weasel their way into positions of influence, while his own father had to work two jobs just to send his kids to college. Life was so unfair!

As the months went by, Alan frequently complained to the staff about the board's ignorance and lack of appreciation for his ideas. He gave a series of lectures during board meetings to try to bring the members up to his level. The relationship between Alan and Barbara continued to deteriorate, hitting an especially rocky patch over the hiring of a new staff member. Alan had found an applicant with impeccable credentials, including a Ph.D. in counseling. Barbara, however, preferred a candidate with fund-raising experience who had been referred by her cousin, the mayor. After lobbying several board members, Alan won this battle and viewed his victory over Barbara as a good sign.

Encouraged by his triumph in the hiring dispute, Alan arranged individual meetings with influential board members to discuss how Barbara might be removed from her position. Although they listened politely, none offered any definite support. In the ensuing weeks, Alan became increasingly obsessed. He stopped talking with Barbara directly but continued to recount tales of her misdeeds to anyone who would listen. The staff was now split into two camps: those who agreed with Alan that Barbara was the root of all evil and those who felt that Alan's obsession with her was hurting the center. Some staff members stopped speaking to one another.

Early one morning, Alan received a phone call requesting his presence at a meeting of the board's executive committee. When he arrived, Alan was told that his employment was being terminated and that he was to pack up his office immediately. The war with Barbara was over. Alan had lost. As he drove away from the Horizon Center, Alan wondered why every place he worked was filled with such stupid, incompetent people.

DEVELOPING POLITICAL INTELLIGENCE

Given his intense dedication to the organization, Alan might be considered a Martyr: while trying to help the Horizon Center succeed, he gradually brought about his own destruction. Toward the end of his tenure, however, he was rapidly moving into the Dimwit category, because his obsession with Barbara was beginning to hurt the entire organization. Alan may have been a visionary, but his political instincts were virtually nonexistent.

Winners often seem to have a "sixth sense" that helps them successfully navigate turbulent political waters. Upon entering a room of complete strangers, they can quickly determine who actually has power and who is just faking it. They get along with even the most prickly people and can bring up controversial issues without provoking or offending anyone. When others play destructive political games, they are able to respond with subtle countermoves; and if they set their sights on a goal, they almost always get what they're after. In short, Winners are blessed with Political Intelligence.

The need for Political Intelligence is universal. Anyone, in any job, can use these skills to make work more productive and pleasant. After years of talking with clients from all walks of life, I have concluded that people from the production line to the executive suite are troubled by similar issues and need similar political abilities. Developing a high Political IQ can help you do many things:

- Clearly define the steps that will lead to your goals
- Recognize the power relationships in any group
- Capitalize on opportunities to increase your personal power and influence
- Identify the true motives and hidden agendas of others
- Remain focused on important objectives and ignore distractions
- Build positive relationships, even with unpleasant people
- Respond appropriately to both devious and direct attacks
- Turn conflicts and arguments into productive discussions
- Avoid wasting energy on irrelevant issues and unattainable goals

Politically intelligent people also know when they should leave a toxic environment and find a healthier place to work.

Although Political Intelligence may be an innate talent for some, most of us sharpen our political acumen through an ongoing process of trial and error. Unfortunately, this learning experience is often painful. The privileged few receive guidance from a wise mentor or trusted adviser, but most people are not so lucky. Fortunately, however, these skills can be taught to anyone willing to examine and change their own attitudes and behaviors. The greatest barrier to becoming a Winner is the inability to see yourself clearly, because self-knowledge allows you to make wise choices about your behavior and avoid political pitfalls.

DEMOCRATIC VALUES VERSUS ORGANIZATIONAL FACTS OF LIFE

The beginning of Political Intelligence is the acceptance of certain realities that we will call Organizational Facts of Life (OFOL). Unfortunately, many bright and talented people, like Alan, fail to comprehend that our deeply held democratic values just do not apply at work. Freedom of speech; liberty and justice for all; government of the people, by the people, and for the people—these are not principles that operate on the job. Clinging to the belief that the workplace should function democratically will only doom you to frustration and disappointment. To excel at office politics, you must understand and accept some fundamental facts:

The Organizational Facts of Life

- OFOL #1: Organizations are not democracies.
- OFOL #2: Some people have more power than others.
- OFOL #3: Virtually all decisions are subjective.
- OFOL #4: Your boss has control over much of your life.
- OFOL #5: Fairness is an impossible goal.

Organizations are power hierarchies, and they are power hierarchies for a reason. If we had to wait for everyone—or even a majority—to agree on a course of action, very little would get done. Some people are therefore given the power to make decisions that others must carry out. Alan got into trouble by failing to accept his place in the power hierarchy and trying to exercise more authority than he actually possessed.

Because some people have the power to direct the actions of others, we are constantly affected by the decisions of those above us. A frequent lament is that their decisions are too "subjective," which is absolutely true. Decisions are inherently subjective because they are made by people—and people base conclusions on their own values, beliefs, goals, and preferences, which may differ from our own. Had you talked with Alan about the conflict over the staff vacancy, he would have told you that Barbara just wasn't being "objective" about it. "If you view the situation *objectively*," he might say, "the correct decision is obvious. My candidate clearly has the better credentials. Barbara's decisions are always so subjective." From her perspective, Barbara would provide a different view: "If we hire someone with fund-raising experience, then she'll be able to help us raise money to expand our services. And knowing the mayor will give her greater access to people at City Hall. We've already got plenty of people with degrees in counseling, but Alan's so entranced by Ph.D.s that he can't view this *objectively*." So here we have two people involved in one decision who each think the other is being too subjective! In fact, the only completely objective decisions are those that involve counting—as in, "Which piece of machinery can produce more grommets per hour?" or "Which plane can hold more passengers?" These questions are so easily answered, however, that we don't really think of them as decisions at all.

Alan also had difficulty with OFOL #4: Your boss has control over much of your life. When we go to work, we trade personal control for pay, benefits, interesting activities, a chance to get out of the house—or anything else that motivates us to take a job. At times, we may regret this bargain and attempt to get some of that control back. To maintain the illusion of control, people sometimes do things that can seem rather obtuse to a neutral observer. George, an executive vice president whose company had just hired a new CEO, is a perfect example of this phenomenon. Because George did not like the CEO, he developed the unfortunate habit of complaining loudly about the CEO's management style to anyone who would listen. Upon arriving at work one morning, George's astonished staff found his office completely bare, with no sign that George had ever existed. He had been fired by the CEO and was never heard from again. Why did George choose to engage in such obviously self-destructive behavior? Because pointing out the CEO's weaknesses made him feel superior and therefore more in control—even though it actually had the opposite result.

Another example, more sad than stupid, is a secretary named Patsy. One afternoon, Patsy was told that her job had been eliminated and that she could come back the next day to pack up her belongings. The following morning, Patsy's boss found her seated at her desk, working away. In a panic, he went looking for the human resources manager. "I don't know what to do," he said. "She's acting as though nothing has changed." When the HR manager spoke with her, Patsy said, "I can't stop now. There are just so many things that I have to finish." In fact, this extreme denial was just helping her maintain psychological control. The reality of losing her job was so frightening that she was clinging to the illusion of being needed.

In Alan's case, the root cause of his downfall was the failure to accept that Barbara was indeed his boss. From the beginning, he resented the fact that she was from a wealthy family, a feeling that probably stemmed from his childhood envy of people with money. He felt superior to her because of his greater management experience and because he viewed his visionary style as more advanced than her concern with policies and procedures. Having to report to her was therefore a blow to his self-image. To feel more in control, he chose to point out her deficiencies and to explain how she needed to change—strategies that would not warm the hearts of many bosses. Barbara quickly got the not-so-subtle message that Alan didn't feel she was qualified to manage him. Unfortunately, Alan completely overlooked the fact that she had more power than he did—both officially, as the board chair, and unofficially, because of her long-standing connections with other board members and her relationship with the mayor. The ultimate Organizational Fact of Life is this:

The person with the most power wins.

Most of the time, the person directly above you in the hierarchy has more power than you do. Your boss can affect your pay, your reputation, your assignments, your advancement, and the general quality of your life. Once you accept this fact, what naturally follows is the need to effectively manage your boss. We usually think of this the other way around: your boss is responsible for managing you and should therefore treat you with respect, courtesy, and—I'll say more about this one in a minute—fairness. But for political success, you need to stop worrying about how your boss treats you and start figuring out how to relate to your boss. The ability to manage upward is an absolutely essential component of Political Intelligence.

One of my personal lessons in boss management came early in my career, when I was hired to work as a management development specialist in a large corporation. At this point, I had several years experience in both management and management training—but in government, not business. Since my new boss was a novice in this field, I looked for any opportunity to demonstrate my superior knowledge. The danger of this approach became apparent when he scheduled a meeting about the new management training program on a day that I had to be out of the office. I was obviously being shut out of this project! From that moment on, I changed my approach and began to communicate with my boss more intelligently—and as a result was able to learn a great deal from him. In my initial arrogance, I overlooked the fact that he had been with the company for fifteen years and knew much more about the business world than I did. Once I stopped being such a show-off, we made a very effective team.

Acceptance of the Organizational Facts of Life is an absolute prerequisite for developing Political Intelligence. Otherwise, you will find yourself constantly agonizing about whether you are being treated "fairly," and fretting about fairness is a complete waste of energy.

THE IMPOSSIBILITY OF FAIRNESS

One surefire way to sabotage your career is to become overly concerned with whether everything is "fair." At first, I felt it wasn't "fair" that my boss left me out of the meeting about management development. Alan definitely felt that having to report to Barbara, a person with much less experience and vision, wasn't "fair" at all. But people with Political Intelligence recognize that perfect fairness is both impossible and irrelevant. Most Western cultures are obsessed with fairness. In the United States, the court system is clogged with cases brought by people who only wish to be treated "fairly." Our language is filled with references to fairness: A fair day's work for a fair day's pay . . . Turnabout is fair play . . . He should have a fair chance . . . She had an unfair advantage . . . Be sure you play fair. If you've raised a teenager—or if you've been a teenager—you probably already know that all children, upon approaching their teenage years, begin to chant the same mantra: "That's not fair!" The universal parental response to this lament is *"Life's* not fair!" As parents (when *we* have the power), we know this to be true—however, at work (where someone else has the power), we immediately forget that life's not fair and begin whimpering about how badly we are being treated.

When we tell our children that life's not fair, we are acknowledging that fairness is truly an impossible goal. There is no absolute standard of fairness because fairness is based solely on perception. Inevitably, therefore, any large-scale decision will be met with a cry of "That's not fair!" from some constituency. For example, suppose everyone in an organization is granted a 10 percent pay increase. Will this universal benefit be perceived as fair? Of course not! People who feel they work harder will resent the fact that everyone is getting the same amount. A "fair" decision would be to either give them more or give those slackers in the next department less—which, of course, would not seem "fair" from their perspective. The most "unfair" decisions are those that simultaneously hurt us and benefit someone else: the promotion that goes to the person who always sucks up to the boss, or the key project given to a less technically competent co-worker who is better at schmoozing. *Their* view, of course, might be different: "I got that promotion because I put a lot of effort into working well with the boss and delivering the results she expects," or "That project requires managing relationships with many different departments. Technical competence isn't enough."

Getting worked up about fairness is a waste of time and politically stupid. People who are obsessed with fairness tend to whine, and nobody likes a whiner. Instead of focusing on the past and complaining about unfairness, start looking toward the future and taking concrete steps to achieve your goals. As we will see in the next chapter, politically intelligent people concern themselves with leverage, not fairness. Leverage is the key to getting what you want, and, if you have enough leverage, fairness is no longer an issue.

Personal Politics

How Good Is Your Relationship with Your Boss?

Assessing your situation:

- Rate your relationship with your manager using the 1–5 scale below.

1	2	3	4	5
I absolutely can't stand my boss.	I manage to tolerate my boss despite our differences.	We're not a perfect match, but my boss is okay.	I get along well with my boss most of the time.	My boss and I have a terrific relationship.

  If your rating is a four or five, be happy! If your rating is below a four, list the problems that you have with your boss. Are these issues interfering with the achievement of your personal or business goals?

- Now, think beyond your own reactions. Would most of your co-workers list the same problems with your boss? If so, do any of them seem to cope with this difficult person better than you do? But if not, why do you have a harder time with this manager than others do? Have you had difficulty with other bosses in the past? Or do the two of you just have very different work styles?

Moving from assessment to action:

- You probably can't change your boss, so you need to figure out what *you* can do to manage this relationship more intelligently: (1) List the situations in which you find your manager's behavior to be most frustrating or annoying. (2) For each situation, list the way that you usually react. How might your behavior make the situation worse? How would your boss describe your behavior? (3) Identify a more productive reaction to these situations. If other people have an easier time with your boss, use them as role models. Set goals for changing your behavior with your boss.

How High Is Your Political IQ?

Assessing your situation:

- Check any of the statements below that might apply to you. The more statements that seem relevant, the more you may need to work on your Political Intelligence.

  □ I am not as effective as I would like to be in influencing others.
  □ I frequently find myself in arguments and disagreements with people at work.
  □ I feel that I have often been treated unfairly in work situations.
  □ There are certain people that I find it impossible to work with.
  □ When I am with a new group, I find it hard to tell where the real power lies.
  □ I am often uncertain about the true motives of other people.
  □ I find that I am easily distracted from important goals by less important tasks.
  □ I find it hard to work with people that I don't particularly like.

☐ I often feel that I am being taken advantage of at work.

☐ If I feel that I am being attacked or undermined by others, I am not sure how to respond.

☐ I get easily upset about matters that are trivial or not relevant to my goals.

☐ Management doesn't recognize the true value of the work that I do.

☐ Certain situations at work may prevent me from accomplishing goals that matter to me.

Moving from assessment to action:

• As you read the rest of this book, keep in mind the items that you checked. Each of them will be addressed in the chapters that follow. As you think about these issues, your task will be to identify the attitudes or behaviors that *you* need to change to improve your situation.

Are You Too Concerned with "Fairness"?

Assessing your situation:

• Divide a sheet of paper down the middle. On one side, list everything about your work situation that you feel is unfair. How many of these items are related to one of the Organizational Facts of Life?

Moving from assessment to action:

• On the other side of the paper, list anything that *you* personally might do to affect the things that seem unfair to you. If these issues are important enough, then start taking action to change the situation. However, if you *can't* think of any way to change it, or if it's not worth your time, then forget about it! Let it go! Any time spent focusing on this unfairness is just a waste of energy that could be more productively directed toward achieving your goals.

Chapter 3

Forget Fairness, Look for Leverage

One sunny Saturday morning, Eric sat on the front porch with his wife, Marcia, waiting for the movers to arrive. They were excited and happy, eagerly anticipating the first day in their new home. A few hours later, however, their mood had changed. The movers had shown up an hour late with a truck too small to hold their belongings. To make matters worse, the workers appeared to be completely untrained. After unloading half the furniture at the new house, one of them dropped an antique desk, smashing it to pieces. For Marcia, this was the last straw. She called a manager at the moving company and threatened to withhold part of their fee because of poor service. The manager then radioed the truck and, on his instructions, the movers locked the van, refusing to unload any more furniture until they had a check for the full amount.

So what does this sad little tale have to do with office politics? Nothing, really—but it is one of the clearest examples I've seen of a leverage miscalculation. Had Marcia been thinking straight—and not overcome with anger at the movers' incompetence—she would have realized that she was pulling a power play at the wrong time. If her goal was a reduced bill to compensate for lousy service, she would have been in a much better position to discuss it once all the furniture was off the truck.

Political Intelligence requires a thorough understanding of the dynamics of **leverage**, which simply means your ability to get others to do what you want. If this conjures up visions of people jumping to obey at the crack of a whip, you've got the wrong view of leverage. Those who try to control others through abusive power and authority usually fail in the long run—or someone stabs them in the back at the first opportunity. When you increase your leverage in more appropriate ways, though, you can be a Winner in the game of office politics—and in other areas of life as well.

Most of our transactions involve leverage in one way or another. Imagine, for example, that you plan to ask your boss for a raise. Are you more likely to get it if you (a) have been a loyal employee for five years or (b) have another job offer? Clearly, your leverage increases if your services are desired elsewhere. Or suppose you want to get a co-worker to help you with a project. Is assistance more likely to be forthcoming if (a) you have helped this colleague in the past; (b) this colleague is going to need your help in the future; or (c) large bonuses will be paid to project participants? The answer is all of the above. Option (c) might be the most effective, but (a) and (b) would increase your leverage as well. Leverage also rears its head in personal relationships. Let's say a guy wants to take off for a two-week hunting trip in Montana with his buddies. Is his wife more likely to agree to this plan if (a) they just spent a romantic weekend at the beach together or (b) he's been working seventy hours a week for the past three months?

CALCULATING THE LEVERAGE EQUATION

The ability to assess your leverage relative to others' is a fundamental aspect of Political Intelligence. In one Dilbert cartoon, a colleague who orders Dilbert to help him winds up with a trash can on his head. "This is where we learn," says Dilbert, "that you are my co-worker, not my boss." In other words, you don't have the leverage to tell me what to do. Winners are able to accurately calculate the **Leverage Equation** in any given situation. Even if you've never used the term "leverage," I'll guarantee that at some level you are aware of the Leverage Equation that is always hovering in the background. If you receive bad service and ask to speak to the manager . . . if you tell the traffic cop that you're friends with the Police Chief . . . if you copy your uncooperative colleague's boss on an e-mail . . . you are simply trying to increase your leverage.

One of the most politically hazardous mistakes is the **leverage miscalculation**. Marcia's transaction with the movers provides an excellent example of this blunder. Her power lay in the fact that she hadn't paid them yet; however, since they were still in control of her furniture, the movers had an equal amount of leverage. Marcia was too angry to realize that as soon as the truck was unloaded, the Leverage Equation would have shifted in her favor.

Leverage miscalculations often create unanticipated (and usually unpleasant) consequences for the lower-leverage person. In the following true stories, consider how these poor unfortunates either failed to assess the Leverage Equation correctly or chose to ignore it.

- Brian, an engineer in a large technology company, was asked by his manager to provide regular status updates on certain projects. Because Brian didn't like his boss and didn't like doing status updates, he ignored this request. As a result, he was described as "uncooperative" on his performance review, lowering his rating and reducing his pay increase. Brian saw this as further evidence that his manager was a jerk. When asked why he didn't simply give his boss the information, Brian replied, "I guess I just don't think I should have to do that." As a person with free will, Brian can certainly choose to withhold information if he wants to. But in the real world, if you choose to defy people who have power, you shouldn't be surprised by the predictable results.

- Lucy, a regional director in a state mental health agency, was responsible for several county mental health centers. Although the center managers reported to her, their funding came largely from their counties, not the state. For that reason, each center was also overseen by a county board of mental health. Glenda, one of the center managers, had been active in county politics for many years, even holding a seat on the county commission. In Lucy's view, Glenda was a loose cannon and something of a management problem, because she routinely made exceptions to policies and failed to follow standard procedures. Every time Lucy brought up one of these issues, Glenda just said, "Well, I'll see what the county board thinks about it." Then Lucy would get a call from the county board chair telling her that Glenda was doing a great job and reminding her that the county provided most of the money for the center. Glenda, of course, continued behaving as she always had. The moral of this story is that being the boss doesn't necessarily mean that you have the most leverage.

- John, a vice president of human resources, was less than excited about the new company president, but he had developed a friendly relationship with Wanda, the president's executive assistant, who had come to the company with her boss. John often complained to Wanda about the president's lack of industry knowledge and changes he was making within the company. She would listen politely, never expressing agreement or disagreement. When the president fired him, John was stunned. He had stupidly failed to consider that Wanda's loyalty to her boss would cause her to pass along John's critical comments. Loyalty is always part of the Leverage Equation. Whether or not people repeat your negative remarks usually depends upon where their loyalty lies.

Leverage miscalculations are not limited to individual issues: entire departments or work groups may fail to assess their leverage accurately. When pilots at a major airline received significant wage increases after threatening to strike, flight attendants decided to follow their example. They went on strike and refused to return to work—but instead of getting raises, the flight attendants got pink slips. Lower-paid workers were hired to fill their positions. These unfortunate employees lost their jobs because they failed to realize that flight attendants simply don't have the same leverage as pilots. Why? Because new flight attendants can be hired and trained much more quickly.

Senior managers, who are accustomed to having a great deal of leverage, may be blindsided when circumstances alter the usual Leverage Equation. In another interesting airline example, executives at a major carrier that was teetering on the brink of bankruptcy decided to award themselves huge bonuses right after asking their unions for large pay concessions. The resulting furor caused the CEO to rescind the bonuses and publicly apologize. But that wasn't enough to appease irate employees and, shortly thereafter, the CEO resigned. This otherwise intelligent man had obviously underestimated (or overlooked) the leverage of the unions during a financial crisis.

Undesirable outcomes created by inaccurate leverage assessments can range from embarrassing blunders to political catastrophes. To help you avoid such problems, the table below summarizes some of the factors that can operate to increase or decrease your leverage.

Sizing Up Your Leverage

You have MORE leverage if you ...	You have LESS leverage if you ...
• Have a higher position • Have more occupational status • Have something the other person needs • Are the sole provider of a resource • Have influence with people in authority • Have abilities that are hard to replace • Have other ways to get your needs met • Have a good reputation or track record • Have less emotional attachment • Have a positive relationship with the other person	• Have a lower position • Have less occupational status • Do not have anything the other person needs • Have strong competition • Do not know people in authority • Have easily replaceable abilities • Are dependent on the other person • Have a poor reputation or no track record • Have a greater emotional attachment • Have a poor relationship with the other person

To make a politically intelligent decision in any situation, you must calculate the Leverage Equation accurately. Overestimating your own leverage to gratify your ego will just set you up for an eventual fall. But if you underestimate your leverage out of modesty or self-doubt, you will miss opportunities to influence others and make progress toward your goals.

LEVERAGE IS DYNAMIC

To keep up with changing political tides, you must always be on the lookout for **leverage shifts**. These power fluctuations occur frequently, both at work and in our personal lives. As children grow from toddlers to teenagers to adults, for example, leverage gradually shifts away from the parents toward the child. Controlling parents who fail to recognize this change will have a tough time when their kids grow up. Leverage can also shift in romantic relationships. If one partner begins to lose interest, the other automatically loses leverage. Misguided attempts to regain leverage by clinging and begging will just make the abandoned partner look weak and pathetic, reducing the poor soul's leverage even further.

In the workplace, leverage shifts happen whenever there are promotions, demotions, or reorganizations. Getting a new boss can trigger a leverage earthquake—and create a great deal of stress. When a new manager comes in from the outside, having no prior history with the group, all bets are off. Everyone starts from zero and must prove themselves all over again. I witnessed one such dramatic shift when a new vice president assumed control of an information systems department. Under the previous VP, the systems director had been the shining star, while the operations director had received a letter of reprimand. But after a few months under the new boss, the operations director was given more responsibility and the systems director was laid off—a complete leverage flip-flop.

When someone is promoted from within the group, leverage shifts may be more predictable. People who were regarded as helpful and cooperative colleagues are now likely to become trusted and valued employees, while former rivals and adversaries may find themselves out of the loop. Sometimes, though, even amiable co-workers can have difficulty with this change. Ed and Tamika worked well together as program specialists in a government organization. After Ed was elevated to the director position, however, Tamika became increasingly uncomfortable with their new relationship. She felt that Ed treated her differently from the new program specialists he had hired. He often questioned her decisions and seldom implemented any of her suggestions. After concluding that their previous work history had actually reduced her leverage, Tamika chose to leave for a position with another agency.

Because dramatic leverage shifts can occur unexpectedly, political Winners follow this principle:

Never intentionally offend anyone at work.

This does *not* mean that you have to suck up to everyone, stifle your opinions, or become the Little Mary Sunshine of your office. But you should learn to work with people that you don't particularly like and handle conflicts in a constructive adult manner. Back in my corporate days, I had a boss who should have learned this lesson. Jonathan, the vice president of my department, was constantly at odds with Sam, one of the division general managers. He played power games with Sam, refusing to share information or involve him in decisions. Imagine Jonathan's surprise when Sam was made president of the company, thereby becoming his boss.

Leverage shifts can occur for a host of reasons—changing market conditions, increased competition, new laws or regulations, or the election of a different political party. Winners stay alert for impending changes, allowing them to anticipate shifts and react appropriately, but shortsighted people who either fail to recognize a leverage shift or stick with outdated approaches may eventually find themselves in political Siberia.

LEVERAGE VERSUS FAIRNESS

When reading some of the examples, you may have found yourself thinking, "But that just doesn't seem fair." And I can assure you that the people involved would agree wholeheartedly—but so what? "Fairness" seldom determines what happens to you at work—leverage usually does.

Low-leverage people spend a lot of time thinking, talking, or complaining about unfair treatment, unfair policies, or unfair management. When I was human resources director for a large corporation, Alvin was one of the "boomerang people"—my term for those chronically unhappy employees who predictably came back with new problems on a regular basis. Every couple of months, Alvin would storm into my office complaining about his boss, his co-workers, his work assignments, company policies, company benefits, or some other issue. Compared to his unfortunate colleagues and managers, I was lucky; they had to deal with this litany of grievances on a daily basis. One of Alvin's complaints was that, although he did good work, he never got promoted. The sad truth was that he actually was a bright, creative person whose work was indeed quite acceptable—but his constant complaining about "fairness" issues made people try to avoid him. When no one wants to work with you, your opportunities for advancement are definitely limited.

High-leverage people don't obsess about fairness. Instead, they remain focused on actions that will move them toward their goals. Vivian, an accounting manager, showed how high-leverage people respond to difficult situations. During her first two years on the job, Vivian received frequent recognition for her efforts to turn around a failing department and modernize corporate accounting practices. Then she got a double dose of bad news: First, the manager who had been her mentor left the company, and Vivian began reporting to a new boss whose last-minute changes drove her crazy. Next, the HR manager informed her that her own leadership style had generated a number of complaints from the accounting staff. Because Vivian was a fast-track achiever who had never known anything but success, this was a real blow. She spent one long, depressed weekend lying around the house, obsessively going over the things her staff had said, and wondering if she should just look for another job. But by Monday morning, she had made up her mind to take charge and correct the situation. She met with the staff to discuss their concerns, formulated a strategy to address the issues, and discussed her plan with the HR manager. She also took the initiative to sit down with her new boss and clarify the way that they communicated about changes. As the situation improved over the next few months, Vivian's credibility as a manager actually increased, because she had proven that she could handle a difficult situation in a positive manner.

USING YOUR ENERGY WISELY

Every morning, you start the day with a fresh supply of energy. By the end of the day, you will have spent that energy allowance on something. You can choose to focus your energy in ways that will increase your leverage and help you reach your goals—or not. Kim Su was a talented information technology specialist who liked tackling new challenges. When people from various parts of the company asked for help with computer problems, she always responded eagerly. Unfortunately, serving other departments was not actually part of her job, so these outside requests often kept Kim Su from meeting deadlines on her own projects. Even though this problem was repeatedly pointed out by her supervisor, Kim Su continued to do the outside work that she enjoyed. When one of her colleagues was promoted to senior IT specialist, Kim Su was upset and complained that she should have been promoted as well. If promotion was her goal, however, she needed to make wiser decisions about where she focused her energy.

Low-leverage people tend to waste a lot of energy on complaining, worrying, blaming, gossiping, scheming, and whining. High-leverage people focus their energy on producing results and building relationships. They concentrate on positive goals and things they can control. After learning about her staff problems, Vivian, the accounting manager, took the high-leverage approach of exploring the issues and identifying changes she could make. Another manager, Chuck, demonstrated a low-leverage response to a similar situation. When an employee survey revealed that his staff had a poor opinion of his leadership skills, Chuck called the employees together, berated them for disloyalty, and told them that he'd be watching them carefully in the future. Word of this tongue-lashing spread quickly through the organization, eventually reaching the president, who was not at all pleased. By allowing anger to drive his response, Chuck succeeded in simultaneously reducing his leverage with both upper management and his employees, demonstrating a remarkable degree of political stupidity.

Sometimes you can turn a negative situation to positive advantage by consciously deciding to redirect your energy and refocus your attitude. Mario was one of several customer service technicians who handled phone calls from customers having technical problems. Historically, calls from particularly angry or upset customers had always been transferred to the supervisor of the department. When the supervisor decided to delegate this responsibility to the technicians, they reacted angrily, complaining behind his back that their boss was just trying to escape work he didn't like. (I'm sure that the phrase "It's not fair" was uttered at some point in this discussion.) Mario joined in the griping at first, but after a few days he decided to view the change not as a burden, but as an opportunity. Because he wanted to eventually become a supervisor himself, this new responsibility looked like a chance to demonstrate his ability to handle difficult customer situations. Mario assumed a leadership role by convincing the other technicians that their wisest course would be to stop fighting the change, draft some guidelines for handling these challenging calls, and present them to the supervisor. This cooperative attitude definitely increased Mario's leverage with management and made the job change easier for his coworkers as well.

Different political types focus their energy in different ways. Sociopaths devote their efforts exclusively to fulfilling selfish desires, while Martyrs exhaust themselves by endlessly striving to meet the needs of others or vigorously championing a cause in the face of constant opposition. Dimwits, who tend to be controlled by their emotions, burn up a great deal of energy satisfying unconscious psychological drives. Chuck probably would fall into this category. Winners, like Vivian and Mario, demonstrate Political Intelligence by refusing to be held hostage by their feelings. Instead, they concentrate on their goals and take actions that will advance both personal and organizational interests.

LEVERAGE BOOSTERS

If leverage is the political wonder drug, you're probably wondering how you can get more of it. Unfortunately, you can't promote yourself to a position of absolute authority, so you'll be glad to hear that politically intelligent people have many options for increasing their leverage. Certain behaviors and characteristics are universal power-boosters.

The Power of Results: Delivering results that make your organization more competitive, effective, or efficient is guaranteed to increase leverage, particularly if you manage to amaze or delight key decision-makers in the process. Should you happen to have a job that allows you to close the deal of the decade or design a brilliant new generation of products, then you are one giant step ahead in the leverage game. But the Power of Results is not limited to people in "glamour positions." You simply have to figure out how your particular job affects your organization's success, then look for creative contributions. A retail clerk, for example, created a new way to display merchandise that increased sales of certain products by 200 percent. The more dramatic the results you produce, the more leverage you will acquire.

The Power of Knowledge: Developing impressive expertise in your work—no matter what job you hold—will cause people to view you as a source of information and a valuable resource. Expertise is especially critical in "specialist" positions—jobs that exist primarily to provide in-depth knowledge of a certain field, such as law, compensation, information systems, and so on. But the Power of Knowledge is not the exclusive property of specialists.

Customer service reps, for example, acquire a great deal of data about customer problems and preferences. Administrative assistants are often invaluable sources of information about practical shortcuts for getting things done. Receptionists who chat with customers and vendors often pick up interesting facts. Anyone, in any job, can acquire useful knowledge to share with others.

The Power of Attitude: But, you say, "I'm just a cog in the corporate machine. I really don't see how I can acquire influence through results or knowledge." Don't despair. You can boost your leverage simply by being the type of person with whom other people like to work—consistently friendly, helpful, and cooperative. The Power of Attitude is particularly evident in the way people react to adversity, so even if you feel cheated, overlooked, or unappreciated, try to keep your negative emotional reactions to yourself. When you have concerns, strive to address them in a calm and professional manner. Dumping all your true feelings on people is a guaranteed leverage killer. (Anyone who believes that complete emotional honesty is a virtue definitely lacks Political Intelligence.)

The Power of Empathy: Most people appreciate a sympathetic ear. As an organizational psychologist, I often find that clients benefit from simply being able to talk about work issues with someone who feels safe. Not that you should strive to become the Dear Abby of your department—that would be counterproductive— but genuinely trying to understand and appreciate others' problems shows that you are not solely concerned with yourself. Beverly, a human resources specialist, was widely known as the person to see if you were having issues with your manager or, as a manager, if you had issues with employees. She was always willing to listen and help people figure out what to do. As a fringe benefit, Beverly gained a great deal of information about what was going on in the company—and that, too, can increase leverage. Of course, you do have to keep any confidences to yourself. Sharing secrets is one way to ensure that eventually no one will trust you.

The Power of Networks: Political Intelligence involves building positive relationships—so it logically follows that Winners increase their leverage by maintaining helpful connections with as many people as possible. Your network is simply the sum total of all the people you can call on for information, assistance, or advice—and this "relationship power" is available to everyone in unlimited supply. The more connections you have—both inside and outside your organization—the greater your ability to get things done and therefore the higher your leverage. As an added bonus, if you ever decide that your best political strategy is to exit for a better situation, your external network will improve the odds of your finding a desirable job elsewhere.

The Power of Inclusion: Involving others in your decisions, activities, and projects can increase support and produce better outcomes. If you happen to have a somewhat solitary nature, becoming more inclusive is definitely a strategy that you should consider. Winners not only take steps to enhance teamwork in their own area, but also try to build bridges to those in other functions. Unfortunately, people seem to have a natural tendency to gravitate toward those similar to themselves, often creating functional or departmental silos. By helping to break down barriers, you will not only increase your leverage, but will also make the business more successful.

The Power of Detachment: Although feeling passionate about your job is a plus, too much passion can be dysfunctional. Dedication to your work may make you credible and persuasive, but those who are too emotionally invested in their jobs can become defensive and inflexible. People who overreact to critiques or constructive suggestions tend to be difficult to work with, so the ability to disengage emotions and view issues objectively can increase your influence. When you develop a reputation as an unbiased and thoughtful observer, others are more likely to seek you out for consultation. As more people consult you, your leverage will increase.

Personal Politics

How Much Leverage Do You Possess?

Assessing your situation:

- Using the chart below, rate yourself on the leverage boosters discussed in this chapter.

Leverage Boosters	Definitely	Somewhat	Not Really
Results: I produce results that provide a clear benefit to my organization.	3	2	1
Knowledge: I possess information that is quite useful to my organization.	3	2	1
Attitude: I am viewed by almost everyone as helpful and cooperative.	3	2	1
Empathy: People often come to me for help with their problems or concerns.	3	2	1
Networks: I know many people throughout my organization.	3	2	1
Inclusion: I typically try to include other people in my decisions or projects.	3	2	1

Leverage Boosters	Definitely	Somewhat	Not Really
Detachment: I am known as someone who can view situations objectively.	3	2	1
Total Points			

A score of 18–21 indicates that you possess a great deal of leverage. Good for you! You should be able to get a lot accomplished. A score of 11–17 shows that you clearly have opportunities to increase your leverage if you choose. If your score is 10 or below, you definitely have some work to do.

Moving from assessment to action:

- If your score is lower than you would like, identify the categories in which you could improve. What are the specific steps you could take to increase your leverage in those areas? What could you do differently in terms of your actions at work or your interactions with people?
- How are you using your energy at work? Are you concentrating on activities that will help you achieve your goals or wasting energy on low-leverage behaviors? How might you need to refocus?

What Leverage Problems Do You Have?

Assessing your situation:

- Can you think of a situation in which you *miscalculated your leverage*—that is, you either underestimated or overestimated the amount of leverage you had? What was the outcome? Does this often happen to you?

- Think about the last time a management change or reorganization created a *leverage shift* at your workplace. How did it affect you? Do you find that leverage shifts often create problems for you?

Moving from assessment to action:

- If you have identified previous problems with leverage shifts or miscalculations, revisit those situations. How would you handle them differently if you could do it over again? What advice would you give yourself for handling such situations in the future?

Chapter 4

Political Psych 101:
Allies and Adversaries

"What you do doesn't matter around here. It's all about who you know." That pearl of wisdom usually pops out whenever someone feels they have been unfairly denied some desirable benefit—a promotion, a raise, a choice assignment, or whatever. And, in fact, this popular rationalization actually is half true. Politically speaking, your good fortune depends upon both what you do and who you know—or more accurately, who knows you. Doing a sorry job will eventually damage your reputation, regardless of your personal popularity. On the other hand, producing absolutely brilliant work will get you nowhere unless the right people know about it.

Remember, virtually all decisions are subjective. So for decisions to go your way, you must be well-regarded by those who are subjectively making them. That's why all Winners know and respect this important political truth:

Positive relationships build political capital.

When you like people, you naturally want to help them. But if you don't like someone . . . well, let's just say you probably won't be found in that person's cheering section. Supporters and allies increase your leverage; enemies and adversaries reduce it. Should your adversaries ever outnumber your allies, you're toast. Even top executives need allies. I once worked with a CEO who alienated everyone he encountered, from secretaries and production workers to the company's largest customers. Although he produced excellent financial results, the board finally decided to fire him. Despite his lofty position, this executive's leverage completely evaporated due solely to his inability to work successfully with other people.

The more allies you have, the more you can accomplish. But don't be naive. To successfully play the political game, you also have to recognize your adversaries. In sports, opponents are easily detected by the color of their uniform. If you're wearing red, you can bet that the guy in blue won't be passing you the ball. You might have a beer together later, but during the game you clearly have conflicting interests. When he wins, you lose. Unfortunately, business relationships are seldom this obvious. If they were, the corporate playing field would be much easier to navigate.

RECOGNIZING YOUR SUPPORTERS

Allies provide you with information, advice, assistance, and support. They are your most valuable political asset. When you are up against a dangerous opponent, having a reliable network of supporters can literally save your occupational life. Shortly after Brad hired Megan as a software designer, he felt that he'd made a big mistake. Her creative ideas and lively banter, which had seemed so appealing during her job interview, soon began to get on his nerves. She appeared incapable of completing a single thought before bouncing off on a different tangent. Whenever Brad looked for Megan, she had wandered off somewhere to talk with someone about something. To make matters worse, she consistently ignored every suggestion that he made. So when the company decided to lay off 10 percent of its workforce, Brad was relieved: this looked like a painless way to get rid of Megan without actually firing her.

Shortly after submitting Megan's name as a layoff candidate, however, Brad received a visit from his boss. "Surely you don't want to lay off Megan!" exclaimed the boss. "She's a real breath of fresh air around here." Megan, it turned out, had not only developed a friendly relationship with her boss's boss, but had also done an excellent job on several high-profile projects. Because people in many departments liked her and were impressed with her work, Megan's reputation had been enhanced through positive word of mouth. Even the CEO questioned why her name was on a layoff list, since he had heard only good things about her. Megan had developed a strong network of helpful allies. Whether this was the result of her natural work style or a calculated political strategy, the effect is the same: Megan has enough leverage to protect her job, at least for now.

Allies can be grouped into three categories: Friends, Partners, and Connections. **Friends** are colleagues who "click" because of common interests or similar temperaments. They simply like each other, for reasons unrelated to tasks, projects, or goals. As you get to know people, these informal alliances naturally develop. Outgoing types find Friends without thinking about it; solitary people have to make more of an effort. Keep in mind, however, that colleagues usually judge your personality and your competence separately. They can love you dearly, but still think you're a bit of a screwup. Many people have been shocked when their warm and chummy office buddies failed to support them for a promotion or left them off an important project team. If your Friends also believe that you do a great job, they will be much stronger allies.

Partners are colleagues who must depend on each other to accomplish results. Because their goals are linked, the actions of one affect the success of the other. Hospital case managers need information about patients from the medical professionals who work with them. Project team members need for everyone in the group to complete their assigned tasks. Accountants need accurate figures from managers to prepare financial reports, while managers need regular updates from accounting to effectively manage their resources.

Anyone whose outcomes are affected by your actions (or vice versa) is your Partner. No need to go searching for Partners—they automatically come with your job. But because they depend on you, Partners will not become your allies unless they believe that you are both competent and supportive. If you slack off on your work, fail to meet deadlines, or try to undermine them, Partners can quickly transform into adversaries. When Partners are also Friends, work becomes more fun. Even if you don't care much for your Partners, however, you still need to be a cooperative colleague for the sake of the business.

Politically stupid people sometimes mistakenly view their Partners as rivals. Two engineering managers in a technology company had become quite competitive. They seldom spoke to each other and discouraged any interaction between their employees. Unfortunately, both worked in product development, with one in charge of hardware, the other responsible for software. Given this situation, no one should have been surprised when the hardware and software plans for a new product turned out to be incompatible. This setback not only hurt the business, but also torpedoed the careers of these Dimwit managers. Because Partners are potentially powerful allies, they should always be cultivated, never alienated. Should you happen to have a naturally competitive temperament, you need to turn it off if you're working with someone on a common project or trying to accomplish a shared goal. Partners should focus their competitive instincts on exceeding expectations, improving past performance, or outdoing the company's rivals—not on beating each other. When that happens, everyone loses.

Connections are people that you can temporarily hook up with when you need assistance or information. In everyday language, when we say someone "has connections," we mean that they know people who can help them get things done. Last year, my staff and I struggled for weeks with a client's computer system that kept automatically deleting our e-mails as spam. After requests to various specialists and managers failed to help, I finally cashed in my connection with the vice president of information systems and asked him to look into the problem. This VP and I had worked together many years ago, and, although we've never been Friends or Partners, I know him well enough to request an occasional favor. This makes him a Connection. I'm not sure what he did, but the problem was quickly solved.

Sometimes people connect because a united effort is temporarily helpful to both of them. In the world of real politics, for example, senators from opposing parties may unite to sponsor mutually beneficial legislation. Such alliances can be valuable in the corporate world as well, and avoiding them can result in missed opportunities. I recently talked with Daniel, a young product manager who was trying to encourage his company to develop business prospects in China. Because management hadn't been too receptive to his proposal, I asked who else might be enlisted to help sell the idea. "The international sales manager," he replied. "But to be honest, I really don't like him very much, so I haven't talked to him about it." Despite Daniel's reluctance, he needs to connect with this sales guy. Both will benefit if the China project is a success—and without an endorsement from the sales group, Daniel isn't likely to make much headway.

The more Connections you have, the more information you can access and the more problems you can solve. But relationships with Connections are more tenuous than those with Friends or Partners, so they must not be overused. If you ask your Connection for too many favors, you may wear out your welcome and lose the connection altogether.

BUILDING A NETWORK

An experienced human resources manager once made a rather blunt observation: "Shy people get laid off," she said to me. Because I know many talented people who are rather quiet and reserved, I didn't particularly like this statement. Yet although her remark hardly seems fair (there's that "f-word" again), I have to admit that it contains a grain of truth. People who avoid interaction have fewer allies. And people without allies are vulnerable.

True political Winners always have a strong network of Friends, Partners, and Connections. Some develop these associations with little conscious effort, while others do so as part of a deliberate strategy. My friend Scottie, a corporate recruiter, is a natural network builder. Because of her outgoing and gregarious temperament, Scottie meets new people easily and has a large collection of friends and acquaintances. I once asked how many Christmas cards she sends out every year. "About two hundred," she replied. When Scottie left her full-time job to finish graduate school, this extensive network helped her find contract work at several prestigious companies. Another woman I know takes a more strategic approach. Being much less sociable than Scottie, she tries to target specific people she needs in her network. But because she is very curious and loves to ask people questions about their work, a friendly relationship usually develops once she makes a connection.

You don't have to be a flaming extrovert to acquire a useful network. But you must be willing to invest a little time in getting to know your colleagues. Highly task-driven people often see interpersonal interaction as an unnecessary distraction from their "real" work. What they fail to realize is that some of those distracting relationships might actually help them produce better results. When some unexpected catastrophe forces these reclusive souls to communicate with long-ignored associates, conflicts often erupt. Without an established relationship, people quickly start blaming and faultfinding, thereby reducing both the likelihood of solving the immediate problem and the odds of any positive communication in the future. A history of friendly interaction always helps to buffer the unavoidable stresses that accompany a crisis.

Erecting artificial barriers can also keep us from meeting potential allies. These walls are created whenever we congregate only with others of our own kind. **Clustering** happens when people habitually group themselves according to some demographic characteristic—age, gender, race, nationality, and so forth. Whenever I speak to a new group, I'm on the lookout for clustering. If all the women sit at one table and the men at another, that's a bad sign. Substitute African-American/Caucasian, Chinese/Korean, middle-aged/young, or a variety of other dichotomies in the preceding sentence, and you have the same result. **Layering** is a similar phenomenon based on organizational level. Apart from necessary work communication, executives talk mostly with other executives, managers with managers, professionals with professionals, and so on. **Occupational tunnel vision** occurs when people ignore everyone and everything outside their own department or function, giving them an extremely limited view of the business.

Interacting with clones of yourself may feel safe and comfortable, but such exclusiveness severely restricts your opportunities. Those who loudly complain that "it's just who you know" are usually the same ones who never take the initiative to get to know anyone. So how do you go about building useful alliances? You can start by developing some new habits—and possibly some new attitudes.

- **Identify the people you need to know.** The most important allies are those who can help you achieve your goals. If you want a promotion, do you know the managers who will be approving that decision? If you want to transfer to another department, do those people have any idea who you are? If you want to change occupations, have you tried to talk with people in your desired line of work? Decide where you want to go, then figure out who can help you get there.
- **Seek out opportunities for interaction.** There is absolutely nothing wrong with sitting at your computer all day or spending your lunch hour reading a book. But you won't get to know anyone that way. Having identified people

who might help you get to your goals, you now need to figure out how to talk to them. Could you make an appointment to discuss some aspect of their work? Or yours? Do you ever run into them in the cafeteria? Would it help to join a professional association? Attend a workshop or seminar? My first management job came about simply because I sat next to an executive at a conference and struck up a conversation. Six weeks later, he called to ask if I'd be interested in working for him.

- **Try to attract people, not repel them.** If your colleagues duck into the restroom when they see you coming, you'll have difficulty building a network. People should view you as a bright spot in their workday, not the low point. Think about the people that you most appreciate at work. How would you describe them? Perhaps you're thinking of adjectives like competent, helpful, friendly, cheerful, interesting, pleasant, and so forth. For network-building, that's who you want to be.

- **Strive for predictability.** Jekyll and Hyde personalities are stressful to be around. If your mood shifts wildly from day to day, people have no idea what to expect. I know one manager with a distinctly bipolar temperament: when she's up, she's cheerful and fun and exciting and friendly—but when she's down, she's dissatisfied and depressed and angry. On any given day, there's no telling which person will appear, so her staff and colleagues tend to be quite cautious until they're certain that she's in a happy frame of mind.

- **Get outside your comfort zone.** People who hang out with their own kind usually have a fear of the unknown (although they probably wouldn't describe it that way). But if you take a risk and make an effort to talk with those "different" people, you will usually find that they welcome your interest and attention. Try having lunch with somebody new. Or meet with colleagues from another department to learn about what they do. Invite people above or below you in the hierarchy to give you some feedback. When you step outside your safe and familiar circle, you may be surprised by how much you learn.

- **Look for links.** Alliances usually develop from shared interests, experiences, or opinions. Finding these "links" can personalize a relationship and establish a basis for future conversation. Do you both have kids? Pets? Do you come from the same part of the country? Like to travel? Have a similar work background? Learn to notice what people talk about and ask appropriate questions. One word of caution, though: avoid potentially offensive topics like religion and politics unless you have clear evidence that the other party either shares your views or enjoys heated emotional debates.
- **Be helpful to others.** A "not in my job description" attitude will most definitely alienate potential allies, especially those who are your natural Partners. Offering assistance builds bridges, so look for opportunities to help. Can you pitch in when they're overloaded? Share useful information? Demonstrate a more cooperative approach? Show a willingness to compromise? If you are a strong, independent type, let others help you every once in a while. Most people like to reciprocate.

To succeed, you need allies. No one can accomplish their goals without the participation and cooperation of other people. And having allies just generally makes work easier and more enjoyable.

IDENTIFYING YOUR ADVERSARIES

Wouldn't it be nice if everyone at work was reasonable, rational, open, honest, and aboveboard? Unfortunately, people who live in that particular fantasy world usually have a rude awakening somewhere in their future. Although you don't want to start seeing enemies behind every file cabinet, almost everybody encounters a few adversaries during the course of their career. Political survivors are able to recognize an opponent when they see one and respond in an appropriate fashion.

When you spot a potential adversary, you need to ask yourself three questions. First, be sure that your diagnosis is correct. Is this person an actual opponent or just an annoying and disagreeable personality? Applying the "adversary" label too quickly can create a self-fulfilling prophecy: the aggravating but harmless co-worker notices your less-than-friendly behavior and responds in kind, thereby confirming your suspicions and plunging the relationship into a downward spiral from which it may never recover. All adversaries are bothersome, but not all bothersome people are adversaries. Winners know better than to get thrown off track by difficult people. They just learn how to deal with them.

A true adversary is someone who stands between you and the accomplishment of your goals. To differentiate between an adversary and an annoyance, consider the earlier example of Brad and Megan. Brad found Megan irritating because her work style was quite different from his own, yet both her work and her interpersonal skills were making his department look good. He may have regretted his decision to hire her, but she certainly wasn't an adversary. On the other hand, from Megan's point of view, Brad is definitely an opponent: he wants her gone.

Suppose that, after careful consideration, you decide that someone is indeed an adversary. Now you must consider the second question: What does this person want? Look for possible motives. Your first clue can be found in this fundamental political and psychological principle:

All behavior has a purpose.

We do what we do to get something we want. "But wait a minute," you say. "People do a lot of stupid things that cause them problems." Very true. But if they continue to repeat the behavior, they're getting some sort of psychological payoff. The nit-picking critic may enjoy feeling superior, even though her stinging remarks alienate everyone around her. The nagging micromanager may be comforted by a feeling of control, even though his frequent interference causes many employees to quit. The procrastinator who puts off difficult decisions may be reducing her anxiety, even though the delays inevitably create future problems. Whenever behavior appears counterproductive and motives seem incomprehensible, stop and consider what the person might be gaining.

Categorized by motive, adversaries fall into three groups: focused, emotional, or vengeful. **Focused adversaries** simply want to get their own way and view you as an obstacle. Their opposition is not personal (although it may feel like it). Some are driven by career ambitions: they want a promotion, a special assignment, an expansion of responsibilities. Fran desperately wanted to become the manager of her department. In a misguided effort to showcase her talents, Fran took every opportunity to brag about her accomplishments and criticize her colleagues. Since she was clearly trying to make herself look good by making them look bad, Fran's co-workers quickly tagged her as an adversary. At the extreme, these ambitious fanatics become Sociopaths, who will happily stomp over anyone to advance their careers.

Other focused adversaries are intent upon promoting their own point of view, without regard to the concerns or needs of others. Many of these folks suffer from a severe case of occupational tunnel vision. I recently met a group of product development specialists who were being held hostage by an engineering manager. They were trying to implement a new cross-functional product development process, but the engineering manager refused to participate. He felt that proper product development could only be done by engineers and that these specialists were infringing on his group's rightful territory. When a meeting was held to introduce the new process, the engineering manager directed his staff not to attend. At a break, one product development specialist encountered an engineer in the hall and asked why none of them were at the meeting. "We have *real* work to do," replied the engineer. "We don't have time for all this useless discussion," clearly illustrating how hostile relationships can develop between entire departments. All too often, this adversarial syndrome is exhibited by people in support functions—such as accounting, human resources, or legal—who become so engrossed in enforcing their own policies that they lose sight of larger business needs. Carried too far, such zealotry can create cause-driven Martyrs, who bullheadedly push their own agenda, refusing to consider other views.

Emotional adversaries are a completely different breed. These poor souls are truly out of control, driven by their intense emotional needs. Underlying their dysfunctional behavior is a deep-seated anger or anxiety that frequently overrides the more logical portion of their brain. One sure sign of an emotional adversary is that the person creates problems for everyone, not just for you. Charlene, the head of a nonprofit organization, was being driven to distraction by her new assistant, Erica. On two occasions, Erica had gotten into shouting matches with another secretary, whom she accused of gossiping about her behind her back. She also refused to interact with anyone from the finance department because they had failed to include her in a birthday luncheon. While leading a group discussion, she began pounding on the table and yelling when she thought people had stopped listening to her. Charlene can coach and counsel Erica till her lips turn blue, but I guarantee that it will make no difference at all: Erica is completely in the grip of her emotions and is unlikely to change without the help of therapy or medication or both.

Not all emotional adversaries are this dramatic. Some play "poor little me," presenting themselves as insecure, vulnerable, and helpless. One such pitiful woman managed to talk her boss out of $1,500 before he realized that she was borrowing money from half the men in the department and never paying it back. Other emotional types specialize in opposition. Rob, a manager in a manufacturing company, simply disagreed with everyone about everything all the time. If you proposed an idea, Rob told you why it wouldn't work. If you remarked that the weather was nice, he said it was going to rain. If you expressed excitement about your upcoming Florida vacation, he warned you about shark attacks. There was absolutely nothing to be gained by talking to Rob. Many people felt he was difficult to deal with, but actually he was quite predictable. For whatever weird emotional reason, Rob was programmed to be contrary. As you may have already gathered, emotional adversaries are often found in the Dimwit category.

More difficult and unpleasant are **vengeful adversaries**, who are unmistakably out to get you—and that means you, personally. If you're lucky, you'll never run into one of these malicious people, but if you do, watch out! Some vengeful adversaries are quite open and direct: they don't like you and you know that they don't like you. Ben, a marketing specialist, intensely resented Greta from the day she was hired. Although their offices were next to each other, he seldom spoke to her and quickly left any conversation that she joined. In meetings, he ignored Greta's comments and belittled her suggestions. He was always on the lookout for her mistakes and frequently complained to their boss about her work. Oddly, Ben didn't act like this with anyone else—in fact, because most people found him to be pleasant and cooperative, Greta had a hard time getting anyone to understand her problem. Although Ben's treatment of Greta never jeopardized her job, he made her life at work pretty miserable.

The most treacherous vengeful adversaries are stealth opponents. Direct confrontation is not their style. These sneaky characters specialize in pointed remarks, subtle challenges, cold shoulders, and disparaging comments. With some, you find yourself feeling uneasy whenever they're around. But with others, you may never even identify them as an adversary until someone else tells you. Or you suddenly find yourself unemployed. Curt was a master of stealth opposition. He was widely regarded as a friendly, jovial guy who was always ready with a quip or a joke, but he had a darker side. After working with Curt in a variety of situations over the years, I began to notice a predictable pattern to his interactions: Curt would develop close working relationships with certain people and become their advocate, frequently "talk-ing them up" to others. But then one of these colleagues would say or do something that Curt interpreted as a personal slight, after which his attitude toward them completely changed. Not to their face, though. With his intended target, Curt was still all sweetness and light. But when talking to others he would make damaging remarks attacking the person's competence or integrity. One of these unsuspecting victims was demoted as a direct result of Curt's smear campaign, and there's no telling how many opportu-nities were lost to the others.

Stealth opponents are vicious. A close encounter with one can make you feel justifiably paranoid for quite a while. If you get wind of their underhanded activities, you can initiate damage control by confronting them directly and taking steps to protect your reputation. Unfortunately, victims often recognize these co-workers as adversaries only after the damage is already done—and sometimes they never learn about them at all.

Adversaries always have an agenda. Some want to do you harm, while others are just self-centered—however, all of them are operating against your best interests. Once you have diagnosed their motives, you must then figure out how to respond.

DEALING WITH ANNOYANCES AND ADVERSARIES

Before considering how to combat adversaries, let's focus for a mo-ment on those who are merely annoying. As you walk through this world, you will encounter people with a wide variety of tem-peraments, personalities, habits, and work styles. That some of them are going to irritate you is a 100 percent certainty. The way you respond to the people you find aggravating is often a good measure of your Political Intelligence. If you let them push your emotional buttons, you will find yourself entangled in unneces-sary and distracting conflicts. But if you stay focused on your goals and keep your logical brain cells working, you can manage the situation to your advantage.

Recently, I was asked to lead a newly formed volunteer organization. One of the members, Martina, quickly offered to help with setting up meetings and coordinating activities. Just as quickly, I began to notice that Martina liked to control and criticize. When I set out materials, she suggested that they be rearranged. When I sat at one end of a table, she suggested that I move to the other end. After attending a social function hosted by another member, she sent me a detailed e-mail listing everything that went wrong. Martina clearly has a little authority problem, but she is also quite dedicated to the group's mission and willing to take on certain activities, like fund-raising, that many members hate. If I get into control battles with her or overreact to her critical comments, I'm going to lose the energy and talents that she can bring to the group. Martina is not an adversary—she's simply a difficult person.

Annoying people represent an exercise in self discipline, but actual adversaries are a different matter. So we come to the last of our three questions: How do you keep an adversary from interfering with your success? First, you must avoid the natural traps lurking in these situations. Then you have a choice: you can try to **convert** your adversaries to allies or take steps to **contain** their destructive potential.

Managing focused adversaries: Because focused adversaries view you as an impediment, their actions can easily lure you into an ongoing power struggle. You need to resist this temptation. A battle for control will just make you seem uncooperative, make others uncomfortable, and make your adversary angry, inviting retaliation. Once a power struggle is under way, someone is probably going to lose. Consider the earlier example of the product development specialists and the engineering manager. After the manager sabotaged their meeting, the product development specialists wanted to go straight to the president and have him order the engineering manager to cooperate. But that approach could create two problems: First, most executives hate being dragged into these cross-functional squabbles. Executives are usually terrible mediators, so they resent anyone who forces them to deal with conflict. Kicking a problem upstairs can therefore cost you some political capital. Second, ratting out the engineering manager to his boss is just going to infuriate him. Infuriated people often become stealth opponents, retaliating in quietly lethal ways that you may never even know about. If the engineering manager has special expertise or highly placed allies, he may have enough leverage to win this power struggle. To solve the problem in a constructive manner, the product development specialists need to take a less confrontational approach.

With focused adversaries, the preferred outcome is to convert them to allies. For this to happen, your opponents must believe that (a) your goals do not conflict with theirs, and (b) cooperating with you might contribute to their own success. To try to convert the engineering manager, the product development folks must first understand his concerns, then convince him that his department is not threatened by their new development process. If he also comes to believe that the new process presents an opportunity for him to shine—or, at the very least, stay out of trouble—then he might be on the road to becoming an ally.

Some focused adversaries cannot be converted, however, and must be contained. Usually, the most effective containment strategy is to increase your leverage, which often involves enlisting the support of those with more power or influence. If an unscrupulous colleague is trying to take over some of your responsibilities, for example, then you probably need to enhance your reputation with key managers. Or suppose that an effort is being made to divert funding from your pet project. Then you'd better start communicating the project's successes and benefits to the right people. If the product development specialists can't make an ally of the engineering manager, then they at least need to contain his hostility and obtain his grudging participation. In fact, that is exactly what happened. The product development group convinced the president that his entire management team needed to take part in implementing the new development process. Once the rest of the executives began to promote cross-functional cooperation, the engineering manager reluctantly agreed to participate. The product development group had thus found a politically intelligent approach to a difficult situation. They never became best pals with the engineering manager, but at least the new process was implemented without a damaging power struggle.

Because forceful adversaries sometimes try to enlarge their territory by pushing into yours, containment may also involve enforcing your boundaries. One of my clients, a mild-mannered young woman named Loren, has a pushy co-worker who frequently inserts herself into others' projects. Loren found this behavior extremely irritating, but the subtle hints that she dropped had no effect (they never do with these people). Finally, after a particularly annoying episode, Loren stepped outside her interpersonal comfort zone and said, calmly but firmly, "Please stop calling my project team members and offering to help them. It only confuses people. If you want to assist with one of my projects, then talk directly with me." The startled co-worker backed off, protesting that she had absolutely no intention of interfering. Some years ago, I experienced a physical example of boundary violation when a rather aggressive colleague walked into my office, came around behind my chair, reached over my shoulder, and picked up the report I was working on. "What's this?" he asked. Meekly answering his question or angrily telling him to back off would have sent the wrong message. I turned my chair completely around to face him, calmly took the report out of his hand, and asked, "Can I help you with something, Mike?" "Not really," he said, then left. I never did figure out what he was after, but with some people, you just have to stand your ground.

Managing emotional adversaries: The key to managing emotional adversaries is to remember that their behavior is triggered not by your actions but by their needs. At work, we generally expect people to act like adults, but emotional adversaries seem more like kids: they throw tantrums, pout, form cliques, play power games, seek attention, or get their feelings hurt. This immature behavior is not limited to a particular person or situation. Most people find them difficult.

The greatest risk with emotional adversaries is that they can "hook" into your own emotional vulnerabilities, causing you to do things that are politically stupid. Nabil, a sales representative, fell into this trap. Nabil was quite successful until he found himself working for Walter, a manager who had the reputation of being suspicious, defensive, and sometimes downright insulting. But at least Walter was an equal-opportunity Dimwit—he was nasty to everyone who worked for him, so most people just put up with his abuse until they could transfer to another district. However, he was a bad match for Nabil, who was a highly anxious person underneath his confident sales-guy facade. When Walter began to criticize everything from Nabil's interpersonal skills to his travel schedule, Nabil went into a tizzy. He took communication classes, signed up for a time management workshop, consulted a personal coach, and even began seeing a therapist. He was spending so much time and energy trying to "fix himself" for Walter that he failed to meet his sales goals, making the situation worse. Walter's criticism had hooked into Nabil's personal anxieties, yanking him out of his usual adult state and triggering a childlike response. Walter's long-standing reputation as a highly critical manager should have been a signal to Nabil to temper his reaction. All those self-improvement solutions are a total waste of energy, because Nabil is not the problem here—Walter is. Nothing that Nabil does will make any difference whatsoever.

Although emotional adversaries can occasionally be converted to allies, containment is usually a more practical goal. Forget about changing their personalities—that would probably require psychiatric or chemical intervention. You simply want to reduce their disruptive behavior, particularly around you. Here's the key: you must control your own reactions, because an emotional response is exactly the reward that this adversary is seeking (albeit sometimes unconsciously). Maintain a calm, rational, adult demeanor, at all times. When an angry outburst produces no reaction, the person will eventually calm down. When a challenging remark is met with a question instead of a comeback, the person will usually stop arguing. When tears fail to elicit sympathy, they will soon dry up. There is one exception to this rule: if adversaries are truly disturbed, with absolutely no control over their behavior, then nothing you do will make any difference. The only solution is to stay out of their way.

When the emotional adversary is your boss, however, damage control requires a Political Game Plan. Nabil, for example, might consider the following steps to remedy his plight with Walter: (1) Accept the fact that Walter is a Dimwit and stop expending energy on useless change strategies. (2) Focus on meeting or exceeding sales goals. Outstanding performance will give Nabil the leverage he needs to counteract any negative reviews from Walter. (3) Strengthen his network of allies, capitalizing on any opportunities to make a positive impression on upper management. (4) Stay calm and focused when talking with Walter, no matter what he says. (5) Be available when needed, but otherwise stay out of Walter's way. No point volunteering to be a target. Of course, if the situation becomes too stressful, Nabil's best strategy may be to seek employment elsewhere.

Responding to emotional adversaries can really test your self-control. During every interaction, you must focus like a laser on your immediate objective and not be distracted by their irrelevant or annoying antics. Don't expect much from them in the way of support. Emotionally driven people are too caught up in their own psychological dramas to be of help to anyone else.

Managing vengeful adversaries: For starters, you should try to avoid creating vengeful adversaries. A few warped people seem to be vengeful by nature, like Curt the stealth opponent, but they are a tiny minority. More often, these adversaries are retaliating for something that you did, perhaps unintentionally. To convert vengeful adversaries, you must first examine your own actions to see what might have triggered their resentment. In one of my early management jobs, I inadvertently created a vengeful adversary for myself. Harry, a member of my staff, had been treated as an informal second-in-command by my predecessor. Because I found Harry to be overly aggressive and somewhat unprofessional, I chose not to continue this practice. To be honest, I really didn't like him very much. As Harry grew increasingly angry about his loss of status, he began to openly question my decisions and criticize my policy changes. I tried to ignore this behavior and treat him like everyone else. Harry didn't have much leverage with either staff or management, so he never created any personal problems for me, but his ongoing dissatisfaction and criticism did nothing to improve the atmosphere in the office. Today, if a client asked me how to handle such a situation, here's what I would suggest: Have a talk with Harry about his previous role and his current career goals. Describe how you see his role changing, but find a way to provide him with leadership opportunities. Give him feedback about his performance as a leader and try to help him succeed. I am almost certain that, had I done this with Harry, he would have become an ally. As it was, he simply maintained his negative attitude until he left for another job.

If you have no idea what you might have done to produce such animosity in your vengeful opponent, try the direct, problem-solving approach. With a rational person, this will usually work if you handle the conversation correctly. You must be sincere in your desire to improve the relationship and nondefensive in your communication. Such a discussion begins with an opening like this: "Ed, I don't think that our working relationship is going very well, and I'm not sure what's causing the problem. I'd like to see if we could figure out how to improve things. What do you think about the situation?" Several things might happen next: Ed may describe the problem, Ed may tell you to go to hell, Ed may wimp out by saying that no problem exists. Whatever his reaction, you must calmly persist until you understand his point of view. Then suggest what you yourself might do differently in the future. After demonstrating your own willingness to change, you should be able to make reasonable requests of the other party. If this approach works, you will have defused an adversary, possibly created an ally, and undoubtedly made your life at work more pleasant.

When your vengeful opponent is not a rational person, however, you need to forget problem solving and go for containment. Focus on protecting yourself from further attacks. Remember Greta, whose colleague Ben had declared war on her for no apparent reason? After an abortive problem-solving attempt, Greta concluded that converting Ben was a hopeless endeavor. No matter what she did, her personality just seemed to annoy and aggravate him. So Greta went into damage-control mode. First, being careful not to trash Ben in any way, she made her boss aware of the problem and described her efforts to resolve the situation, hoping that this might cast a different light on any future attacks by Ben. Next, she tried to strengthen her network of allies by building relationships with other colleagues. Finally, she sat down with Ben and asked him to stop criticizing her in front of others. "I know that you and I disagree about a number of things," she said, "but I would appreciate your talking to me directly instead of making negative comments about me in our staff meetings." This assertive approach conveyed that Greta was no longer going to take the situation lying down. Although the underlying relationship never really improved, Ben did become less overtly hostile and Greta's stress level decreased.

Some adversarial interactions fall into such a predictable pattern that they can be considered a game—although not the kind that you play for fun. Once you spot a game in progress, understanding the pattern can help you choose your next move. The next section begins with a political playbook, including descriptions of common games and suggested strategies for winning.

Personal Politics

How Good Is Your Network of Allies?

Assessing your situation:

- Consider the three different types of allies: Friends, Partners, and Connections. Using the lists below, evaluate your contacts in each of these categories. In each category, check the box that best describes your relationship.

Friends	Partners	Connections
☐ I have friendly relationships with many people at work. We enjoy discussing common interests related to our work activities. We know something about each other's lives outside of work.	☐ I have very supportive relationships with any colleagues who depend on me for results. They regard me as consistently helpful, dependable, and competent.	☐ I know a lot of people that I can call on for work-related information or assistance in getting a problem solved. My network extends into most areas of the organization.
☐ There are a few people at work with whom I discuss common	☐ I have good relationships with some of the people with	☐ I know some people outside my immediate work group that

Friends	Partners	Connections
interests and share information about my life outside of work. However, most of my interactions on the job relate to the business at hand.	whom I work closely, but my relationships with others are not as positive. Some of my colleagues may view me as uncooperative or undependable.	I could call on for information or assistance in getting a problem solved. However, there are a number of areas where I don't know anyone.
☐ Almost all of my conversations at work are about business. I hardly ever talk about my personal life or non-work activities. I may like my colleagues, but I know little about them.	☐ When I have to work closely with others, the relationship often becomes difficult. There are frequent arguments and disagreements. We may try to avoid each other if possible.	☐ I know very few people outside my immediate work group. If I needed a contact in another department, I usually wouldn't know who to call.

- Whose support do you need to accomplish your business or personal goals? Are all of these people in your current network of allies? Do you need to specifically increase your number of Friends, Partners, or Connections?
- If you don't have the allies you need, what has kept you from developing them? The circumstances of your job?

Your own temperament? A tendency to associate only with people like yourself?

Moving from assessment to action:

- Make two lists: (1) people you would like to have as allies with whom you currently have no relationship; and (2) strained relationships that you need to improve if those people are to become allies. Now list the specific actions you could take to develop or improve those relationships.

Do You Have Problems with Adversaries?

Assessing your situation:

- Think about your adversaries. If you believe that you have none, either you are doing a great job politically or you are in denial. If you can identify some adversarial relationships, assess them using the table on page 77. One caution, however: be sure that the person is actually acting adversarial and not just being annoying.

Name of Adversary: _____	
What Do They Want?	**How Should You Respond?**
☐ To accomplish their own goals ☐ To satisfy their own emotional needs ☐ To get revenge for perceived wrongs ☐ To wreck your life	☐ Try to develop a friendly relationship ☐ Initiate a problem-solving discussion ☐ Show that you pose no threat ☐ Stop rewarding their bad behavior ☐ Reduce their influence on others ☐ Increase your own influence on others ☐ Establish boundaries and stand firm ☐ Other?

Moving from assessment to action:

- If you have selected a strategy in the "How Should You Respond?" column, then you need to get more specific about how to implement it. What steps could you take to create a more friendly association? Or what might you do to diminish their influence and increase your own? For the strategy you have chosen, identify your initial action steps.
- Consider whether your own actions or behavior may have contributed to the development of these adversarial relationships. If so, what can you learn from your current situation to prevent such problems from recurring in the future?

Part II

AVOIDING
POLITICAL PITFALLS

Chapter 5

Political Games:
Moves and Countermoves

Ted and Russell were playing a game. Although no one ever announced that a game was under way, all the spectators knew it was on. This game did not have a name or a list of rules, but it did have two opponents and a set pattern of moves. Here's how the game evolved: For many years, Ted had been a human resources director in the largest division of a Southern manufacturing company. Russell, who came from a company in another state, was hired as the new corporate vice president of human resources, thereby becoming Ted's boss. Shortly after Russell arrived, Ted began making pointed remarks about "outsiders who don't understand the company culture"—and thus the game began. Russell's team included the CEO, who had hired him, while Ted's team included the president, a longtime mentor. Over a two-year period, these major moves occurred:

1. Soon after joining the company, Russell implemented several new policies that changed long-standing company practices.

2. Ted, with the president's approval, indicated that he would not be implementing some of Russell's new policies in his division.

3. Russell, with the CEO's approval, reorganized the human resources department. Ted retained his title and salary, but lost most of his staff.

4. Ted was appointed by the president to lead a major project that would normally have been given to the vice president. This was a public humiliation for Russell.

5. Russell contacted an executive recruiter who was also an old friend. The friend arranged for Ted to be offered a higher-paying position in upstate New York.

6. Ted, who had always lived in the South, excitedly accepted the job, moved to New York, and was absolutely miserable in the cold and snow. He never found out that Russell had instigated the job offer. Russell privately declared himself the winner of the game.

During the entire course of this game, no one ever saw Ted and Russell get into an argument or exchange a cross word. In meetings, they were frequently seen smiling and joking with each other. Yet everyone around them knew that a serious game was in progress.

HOW DO YOU KNOW IT'S A GAME?

Political maneuvering is part of the ebb and flow of office life, but games have a specific purpose. A truly malicious game will escalate office politics to an entirely different level. Here are a few signs that can help you spot a game in progress:

- **The players' actions have an identifiable pattern**. Once you spot the pattern, the moves are always predictable. In the Ted/Russell game, the pattern clearly involved mutual attempts at sabotage and retaliation.

- **The behavior has an emotional payoff**. Political games are played for emotional rewards. Each time they made a winning move, Ted and Russell enjoyed feeling dominant and in control, while making the other party feel humiliated and powerless.

- **True motives are never stated**. Political game players always have a socially acceptable explanation for everything they do. Ted and Russell articulated sound, logical business reasons for each decision they made, although the hidden agenda was obvious to anyone paying attention.

- **There is always a winner and sometimes a loser**. The purpose of any political game is to help the player come out ahead. Sometimes, though not always, there is an opponent who must be defeated or humiliated. After each move in the Ted/Russell game, one felt like a winner and the other a loser. Ironically, even though Russell made the ultimate winning move, Ted never knew about it. He just thought that he was leaving the playing field.

- **Any attempt to change the game is met with resistance**. Players will oppose anyone who tries to break the game's pattern, because they don't want to lose the emotional payoff. If their behavior seems silly or self-defeating, keep in mind that emotional reactions can seldom be understood with logical analysis (although emotions do have a logic of their own). Several well-meaning colleagues tried to help Ted and Russell resolve their differences for the good of the department, but both were too focused on revenge to care about any higher purpose.

The most common political games fall into three categories: Power Games, Ego Games, and Escape Games. Keep in mind that these popular pastimes are hardly limited to the workplace. We often play them with family and friends as well!

POWER GAMES

Power Game players are either trying to acquire more leverage or flaunt the power they already have. Some players have malicious intentions, while others are merely self-absorbed. All Power Games are designed to give the initiator some type of advantage over other people.

The Suck-Up Game: "I think you're wonderful, so you have to like me."

Eduardo, a regional director, was meeting with Albert, one of his district managers.

"So what do you think about this new marketing proposal?" said Eduardo.

"Great idea, boss!" exclaimed Albert. "Your plan should send our sales right through the roof!"

"See any problems at all?" Eduardo asked.

"Nope, it looks perfect to me," Albert replied. "Can't wait to get started on it."

At his next staff meeting, Albert shared Eduardo's marketing proposal with the sales staff.

"But how will we ever find time for this?" asked one of the salespeople. "We're short staffed as it is. Putting all this effort into business development is going to keep us from servicing our current customers. We may wind up actually losing business."

"I know it's a problem," said Albert. "But you'll just have to find the time. That's what the boss wants, so that's what we're going to do"

"But did you talk to Eduardo about the potential problems with this plan?" asked another salesperson. "Does he know the risks?"

"I'm not here to criticize management's ideas. I'm here to make them work," Albert replied. "You know my motto: 'Keeping the boss happy is job one.' So we're just going to have figure out how to do this."

Recognizing the Pattern: Suck-Up players direct all their energy upward. They shower managers with compliments, frequently request their guidance, and never openly disagree with them. Advanced players actively seek out opportunities to stroke the egos of important executives.

The Emotional Payoff: "I feel safe when people in power like me."

Pitfalls for Players: (1) Colleagues generally think that Suck-Up players are useless, so they seldom have allies among their peers; (2) when problems occur unexpectedly, managers can become quite unhappy with Suck-Ups who concealed the bad news and failed to provide a warning; (3) if they acquire a manager who wants unfiltered opinions and honest feedback, Suck-Up players are out of luck.

Exposing the Game. You can often disrupt a game by describing the pattern that you have observed or sharing your thoughts about the player's underlying motives. In private conversations with Suck-Ups, the game can be directly exposed by stating your observations: "Albert, I've noticed that in meetings you always agree with Eduardo. You seem reluctant to express any concerns." But if you and the Suck-Up player are in a public setting, asking questions is a less confrontational strategy: "Albert, when we talked about this yesterday, you indicated some concern about the cost. Could you share those thoughts with Eduardo?"

Countermoves: Countermoves are designed to break the pattern of a game, allowing you to get back on a more productive track. With Suck-Up players, the game is generally more annoying than harmful, unless your management is unusually susceptible to flattery. Problems do arise, however, when sucking up prevents the sharing of complete information or honest opinions. Countermoves should therefore be focused on encouraging more candid discussions.

- **Solicit their opinions privately**. To learn what Suck-Ups really think, try talking to them one-on-one. They feel safer expressing opinions (assuming they have any) when management is not around.
- **"Out" them in meetings**. If you know their true views, you may be able to draw Suck-Up players into the discussion with appropriate questions. But not maliciously! Your aim is to get them to share their thoughts, not make them look devious. If you try to trick or trap them, then you are turning into a game player yourself.
- **Don't become their opposite**. Suck-Up players are so compliant and accommodating that their colleagues can look downright cranky by contrast. Be sure that your own comments and suggestions are presented in a positive, helpful way.

The End of the Game: Suck-Up Games end in one of two ways: the player either becomes more assertive and self-confident, or acquires a boss who hates Suck-Ups.

The Control Game: "You can't tell me what to do."

"You'd better watch out," said Sherry's colleague. "I hear that Matt is playing golf with your boss again this weekend." That news sent Sherry into an immediate depression. Ever since he was transferred into her department, Matt had made it quite clear that he had no respect for Sherry and believed he should have her job. He constantly argued with her, frequently ignored her requests for information, and seldom consulted her about any aspect of his work. And now he seemed to be cultivating her boss, occasionally eating lunch with him or joining him for golf outings. "I know that I should do something about this situation," Sherry said to her friend, "but talking to Matt is so unpleasant that it's easier to just leave him alone."

Recognizing the Pattern: Control Game players resist direction or advice from others. Some are dominators, who enjoy telling people what to do. Others are resistors, who may have little desire to lead others, but strongly resent any outside influence over their own activities. Judging by his behavior, Sherry's pal Matt appears to combine both characteristics.

The Emotional Payoff: "I get to do what I want to do."

Pitfalls for Players: (1) Control Games often degenerate into useless power struggles that drain energy from more productive activities. Observers typically wonder why these silly people can't just grow up and get along. (2) Someone usually loses. Although Matt may feel that he's winning this game, he needs to be careful; playing a Control Game with your boss can be risky, because managers automatically have a certain amount of leverage.

Exposing the Game: When exposing a game, you must maintain an adult and businesslike attitude. This means that you can't say everything you would like to say. Sherry, for example, might really want to scream, "Matt, why are you sneaking around and trying to overthrow me, you arrogant little sonofabitch?" Not a good idea. Better to expose the game by saying, "Matt, we need to talk about why you've been ignoring my requests." Or, "I'm getting the message that you don't really like working for me."

Countermoves: In a destructive or adversarial game, effective countermoves can protect the target from possible harm. Here are some strategies to consider if you find yourself facing a Control Game player:

- **Don't get sucked into an overt power struggle.** Responding with vengeful control moves of your own will just bring you down to their level and invite retaliation. You need to guard your territory but remain above the fray, so don't trash your opponent to others or go for an obvious power grab.

- **Stand your ground**. Insecure people often lose Control Games because they give in too easily. If someone is challenging you, you must establish appropriate boundaries and enforce them. When Matt ignores Sherry's requests, she needs to follow up until he provides the information. Otherwise, he gets the message that she's a wimp who can be easily dominated.

- **Fortify relationships with high-leverage allies**. Because Control Games are about leverage, you must ensure that the relevant power people are in your corner. Now that Matt has started cozying up to her boss, Sherry should capitalize on the access to higher-level people automatically provided by her management position. By strengthening the relationship with her boss and looking for opportunities to favorably impress upper management, she can shift the leverage equation in her favor.

- **Directly address problems with the work**. Instead of getting emotionally "hooked" by your opponent's challenging behavior, keep your focus on work-related issues. To initiate such a discussion, Sherry might say, "Matt, I need to get more regular updates about your work. I'd like for us to start meeting once a month to talk about your projects."

- **Go with the resistance**. "Going with the resistance" is a time-tested strategy used by therapists, salespeople, and martial arts experts. Simply put, this means that, when people are pushing you, you don't push back. But neither do you give in; you simply accept their resistance or use it to move the discussion in a helpful direction. For example, if Matt criticizes Sherry's ideas, she doesn't argue. Instead, she might say, "That's an interesting point. I'll keep it in mind." Or, "Tell me what you would suggest."

The End of the Game: A Control Game is over when the relationship stops feeling adversarial and people are working cooperatively, or when the weaker player gives up.

The Shunning Game: "If you don't fit in, we're going to get you."

The six executive assistants at Marcus Corporation were proud of their professional image, viewing themselves as somewhat superior to other secretaries. They tried to maintain a certain "look," with tailored suits, stylish haircuts, and tastefully applied makeup. Every day, the group ate lunch together in the company cafeteria and, once a month, they went out for drinks after work. When they heard that a new vice president was joining the company, the executive assistants looked forward to adding a member to their exclusive little club. But when they met the new VP's assistant, they were dismayed. Darla wore no makeup, dressed in cotton sweaters and ankle-length flowered skirts, and had an unruly mane of long, curly hair. In their opinion, her voice was just a little too loud and her manner a little too casual. Two of the women tried to "help" Darla by telling her where they bought their clothes and got their hair cut, but she just laughed and said, "Hey, you look great, but I'm just a laid-back kind of gal." After a couple of weeks, Darla began to notice that no other executive assistants ever stopped by her desk to chat. At lunchtime, she would suddenly realize that everyone else had left. One day she walked by a conference room and saw the others smiling and laughing as they sliced a birthday cake. Finally, she asked one of her colleagues if she had done anything to offend them. "Why, no, of course not," the other assistant replied coolly. "Whatever made you think that?"

Recognizing the Pattern: Shunning is a group game that requires a target, who is being punished for deviating from established norms. Targets gradually realize that they are being excluded from group gatherings and friendly office banter. Any conversation that they join breaks up rather quickly. Required communication is always cool and formal. But since no one will acknowledge that anything unusual is occurring, all attempts to discuss the problem are brushed aside.

The Emotional Payoff: "We feel more powerful because we can punish people."

Pitfalls for Players: (1) Because it is a childish game, Shunning makes the players appear immature and small-minded; (2) Shunning creates powerful feelings of anger in the target, who may look for opportunities to retaliate. And if the target ever acquires significant leverage, Shunning players better watch out.

Exposing the Game: Shunning can be difficult to expose, because denial of the game's existence is an integral part of the game itself. Strenuous attempts to get Shunning players to admit their tactics will only make the target appear needy and pathetic.

Countermoves: Countermoves to a Shunning Game focus on reducing the target's isolation and gradually breaking down the group's united front.

- **Find other sources of support.** Sometimes the target can simply join another group. Darla, for example, might begin eating lunch with some secretaries outside the executive area.
- **Divide and conquer.** Often the target of a Shunning Game can chip away at the hostile group dynamic by getting to know the friendlier members. Shunning players usually vary in their level of commitment to the game. Typically, one or two leaders are strongly invested in punishing the target, but other members may feel a bit guilty about being so mean. By developing a relationship with these more accessible players, the target may be able to short-circuit the game.
- **Try to define the offensive behavior.** Shunning targets often have no idea what they are doing wrong. Because no one will acknowledge the existence of a problem, they can't fix it. By talking with accessible group members, targets can sometimes identify the cause of their colleagues'

resentment. "I know that something about me bothers the other assistants," Darla might say to a more approachable co-worker. "But I have no idea what it is. I would really appreciate your helping me understand the problem."

- **Change things that are reasonable.** One Shunning target learned that his constant talking was driving his colleagues away. Now, that's a behavior he might want to work on. Darla, on the other hand, should feel no obligation to get her hair cut or start wearing makeup just to please the other secretaries. But if doing so would help her achieve her career goals, she might consider it.

The End of the Game: Shunning Games usually end in one of two ways: either the group offers the target at least minimal acceptance or the target leaves. Shunning is a brutal psychological weapon that can place almost unendurable stress on the victim. Most people cannot tolerate that kind of pressure for long. Nor should they.

EGO GAMES

All Ego Games are designed to make the player feel smarter, better, or more special than other people. Some games require a victim, while others just allow the players to puff themselves up a bit. Most Ego Game players are actually masking strong feelings of insecurity or inferiority.

The Superiority Game: "Aren't you impressed with me?"

Charlotte sat down in her colleague's office for a meeting. "Did you hear about the big project that the CEO has asked me to lead?" she said brightly. "No one has ever taken on anything like this before!"

"Great," replied her colleague. "Now I need to ask you about . . ."

"And do you know what? I'm going to have to go to Japan to meet with our vendors over there," Charlotte continued. "The CEO wants me to be sure that all the contract requirements are being met."

"Terrific," said the colleague. "But we need to talk about . . ."

"Hold that thought," said Charlotte, as she answered her ringing cell phone. "I've got to take this call. It's really important. Let's talk later." The colleague just sighed as Charlotte disappeared into the hall.

Recognizing the Pattern: The words and actions of Superiority players send the clear message that they are important, unique, and indispensable. Hogging the conversation, bragging, and ignoring others' needs are all Superiority moves. When their real life isn't impressive enough, some dedicated players will actually fabricate stories. Superiority usually has only one player, who is simply in search of an audience. But when two players compete, a predictable and pointless "my dog's bigger than your dog" pattern emerges.

The Emotional Payoff: "I can make others believe that I'm important and special."

Pitfalls for Players: (1) Superiority behaviors are quite annoying to colleagues, who eventually just tune out these braggarts; (2) because these maneuvers are rather transparent, Superiority players often come across as insecure—the exact opposite of the impression they are trying to create.

Exposing the Game: This game is easily revealed by verbalizing the player's underlying message. "You certainly seem to have a lot of impressive contacts, Charlotte." Or, "I guess our meeting wasn't really too important compared to the other things you had to do." You must make these statements in a calm and sincere tone. Superiority players are trying to compensate for a lack of self-confidence, so irritation and sarcasm will just hurt their feelings and make the situation worse.

Countermoves: Because Superiority players are just trying to impress their audience, these games are usually more aggravating than destructive. If the player's behavior begins to interfere with the work, however, then it needs to stop.

- **Avoid getting hooked.** Never, under any circumstances, try to top a Superiority player with a story of your own. This just leads to an endless cycle of one-upmanship.
- **Don't reward annoying behavior.** When you ignore self-promoting comments and attempts to control the conversation, these inappropriate behaviors will diminish. But if you ask Charlotte one polite question about her big project, you may waste fifteen minutes listening to her answer.
- **Address problem behaviors directly.** When a Superiority player is interfering with others' performance or productivity, then you should ask them to stop the disruptive behavior. "Charlotte, I need for you to make other arrangements for your calls when we're having a meeting. The cell phone interruptions are making it difficult to have a discussion."
- **Remember the motive.** Anyone who tries this hard to look important doesn't really feel that way. If you can remember that Superiority players are actually quite insecure beneath all that posturing, then you may feel more sympathetic toward them.

The End of the Game: A Superiority Game is over when the player stops trying to impress you and acts like a normal person. Some people will only play Superiority to impress new acquaintances and drop the pose once they get to know you.

The Put-Down Game: "You're obviously an idiot, so I must be brilliant."

George, a manager, had been listening to a staff member's presentation for about three minutes. "Stop right there!" he ordered. "As any fool could see, your conclusions are incorrect. I used to think that you had a mind for strategy, but now I'm not sure that you have a mind at all. That's quite enough." The staff member meekly sat down.

Later that day, a colleague stopped by George's office. "I wanted to see what you thought of my proposal," she said warily.

"Hopeless!" barked George. "Of course, if you want to alienate every single one of our international customers, that would be the way to do it."

"What's wrong with it?" she asked. "I put a lot of work into . . ."

"Well, I certainly couldn't tell," interrupted George.

Recognizing the Pattern: Put-Down Games require a player and at least one target. These players are pathetic little souls who can only feel good about themselves by making someone else feel stupid or inept. They specialize in sarcasm and criticism, making biting remarks that are unnecessary and hurtful.

The Emotional Payoff: "By demonstrating my superiority over others, I can feel less inferior myself."

Pitfalls for Players: (1) Put-Down Games quickly produce resentful and angry adversaries; (2) with their constant belittling of others, these players actually appear insecure instead of superior.

Exposing the Game: The target can expose this game by calmly describing the reaction that the player is trying to produce: "Well, George, I guess you put me in my place." Or, "George, you're obviously smarter than I am." Preferably said with a smile.

Countermoves: Because they are widely known as chronic complainers, Put-Down players are often politically toothless. They are most unpleasant to be around, however, so avoiding them is usually a wise stress management strategy.

- **Don't give them what they want.** Watching you tremble is most rewarding to a Put-Down player, so maintain a self-confident appearance. Always respond calmly to any assaults. Or just give them a dismissive look and continue with what you were saying.
- **Minimize contact.** Why set yourself up for target practice? You should only interact with these attackers when you have no other choice. If you are unfortunate enough to work for a Put-Down player, then just remember that it's your boss who's the Dimwit, not you—and find another job as soon as possible.
- **Get other opinions.** Never evaluate your own work by the reactions of a Put-Down player. Find some mentally healthy people who can provide a more balanced and rational view.

The End of the Game: This game only ends when one of you leaves. Put-Down specialists seldom change.

The In-Group Game: "You'd like to be one of us, but you can't."

Nine district managers from a social services agency are attending their regular quarterly meeting. Every quarter, on the day before the meeting, four of the managers take the afternoon off, for a round of golf. After golf, the same four always have dinner together, then meet for breakfast the next morning. In the meetings, they all sit on the same side of the table and talk among themselves. If one makes a proposal, the other three always agree. They have all been district managers for at least ten years.

On the first day of this quarter's meeting, a new member unknowingly sits in a chair usually occupied by one of the senior four. So many "joking" comments are made about his seating choice that he finally moves to a chair on the other side of the table.

Recognizing the Pattern: An In-Group Game requires two separate and unequal groups. Everyone knows that one group is more desirable and that membership is restricted, but no one is supposed to talk about it. Members of the In-Group share some identifiable characteristic. For the "in" district managers, length of employment seems to be the distinguishing attribute. Unlike Shunning players, In-Group members are not necessarily hostile to the "out" group. They just enjoy being part of their special little clique. Communication between the two groups may be quite cordial and pleasant, but everyone knows that an invisible barrier exists (although members of the "in" clique will never publicly admit it).

The Emotional Payoff: "Being part of an exclusive group makes me feel special."

Pitfalls for Players: (1) Resentment often festers beneath the friendly facade of out-group members, who can easily become vengeful adversaries; (2) divided groups are seldom as effective as cohesive groups, so the work usually suffers along with the relationships.

Exposing the Game: For safety's sake, out-group members need to band together to expose an In-Group Game. A lone individual who attempts to disrupt this entrenched pattern risks being labeled as a deviant and treated accordingly. The reaction to the new district manager sitting in the "wrong" seat is a small example. Collectively, however, members of the out group can expose the game by simply describing it: "We've noticed that the four of you seem to spend a lot of time together. How about giving the rest of us a chance to get to know you a little better?"

Countermoves: The purpose of breaking up an In-Group Game is not to disrupt In-Group relationships, but to make the whole group more inclusive.

- **Bring the issue into the open.** The existence of cliques can often be delicately acknowledged by making observations. "Sometimes decisions seem to have been made before we get into the meeting." Or, "We always seem to be divided into two groups. Why is that?"
- **Build one-on-one relationships.** Out-group members can safely initiate friendly individual relationships without taking on the whole In-Group at once. They may do this by asking for advice, requesting assistance, or just chatting about the weekend.
- **Suggest activities that either mix the groups or include all group members.** Increased interaction often helps to break down cliques. As members become better acquainted, relationships will naturally develop. Strategies may include creating project teams with members from both groups or engaging in group social activities.

The End of the Game: The game is over when all members of the group can interact freely, without feeling that some "rule" is being violated. Unless the In-Group is really entrenched, this goal can usually be achieved.

ESCAPE GAMES

The purpose of an Escape Game is to avoid unpleasant consequences. In the two games described below, players are either actively trying to avoid blame or passively shirking responsibility.

The Scapegoat Game: "This problem was clearly your fault."

The management team of Hudson Enterprises, a chain of women's apparel stores, was glumly reviewing their year-end results, which showed a 32 percent decline in sales from the previous year.

"This is clearly an advertising problem," said the CEO. "Our ads just aren't getting people into the stores."

"But this year's ad campaign was almost the same as last year's," responded the marketing vice president. "And last year sales were great. What changed was the merchandise."

"Yes, but people have to actually come into the stores to buy the merchandise," retorted the CEO. "And the ads just didn't get them in this year."

"In the stores where we measured traffic, plenty of people came in," said the marketing VP. "They just left without buying anything."

"Well, the ads apparently weren't attracting the right customers. So perhaps using last year's campaign was a bad decision," declared the CEO.

"Our typical customer profile hasn't changed for years," said the marketing VP. "We just stopped carrying the kind of clothes that they like."

"The new styles were great!" exclaimed the CEO. "I picked most of those lines myself. You have to keep up with the times. And your ad campaign is outdated." As they left the meeting, the operations executive turned to her marketing colleague. "You might as well give it up," she said. "He's decided that this is an advertising problem, so it's going to be an advertising problem. The facts are completely irrelevant."

Recognizing the Pattern: The Scapegoat Game, which requires a target and a problem, can be played by individuals or groups. In Scapegoat, the target is quickly determined to be the cause of the problem, with no exploration of other possibilities. When Scapegoat is played between colleagues, their blame-shifting conversations sometimes resemble a tennis match. Taken to a higher level, Scapegoat can also be played by entire departments. If your boss is a chronic Scapegoat player, the game can be hazardous, because bosses often have the leverage to punish people. Politically inept players, who try to make their boss a target, usually meet with an unfortunate end.

The Emotional Payoff: "If I'm not the cause of the problem, then I don't have to feel responsible, guilty, or stupid."

Pitfalls for Players: (1) Resentful and angry Scapegoat targets will often try to return the favor when future problems arise; (2) successful Scapegoating usually means that the real issues are never identified, so the problem continues.

Exposing the Game: As with many games, Scapegoat can be exposed by calmly commenting on what seems to be occurring. An observer might simply say, "We seem to be settling on advertising as the only cause of the problem. There may be other contributing factors." Targets, however, will sound less defensive if they use a question: "Do you feel that advertising is the sole cause of the problem?"

Countermoves: In Scapegoat, countermoves are designed to deflect attention from the target, broaden the scope of the discussion, and determine the true source of the difficulty. If you have a boss who likes to play this game, you may have to divert significant energy to ongoing CYA ("cover your ass") activity.

- **Avoid getting into an argument.** Because no one likes being blamed, Scapegoat discussions can turn into heated debates. Targets, who feel with some justification that they are being unfairly attacked, often respond in kind, turning the discussion into a free-for-all.
- **Acknowledge the possibility of partial responsibility.** To avoid appearing defensive, targets may volunteer to as-

sume some portion of the responsibility. "It's possible that advertising could have played a role, so I'll look into that and report back at the next meeting. But there may be more than just one factor at work here."

- **Defend yourself subtly.** Without firing back directly, try to incorporate a line of defense into your response: "Well, we did use the same ad campaign as last year, but it might not have worked quite as well with this year's merchandise."

- **Broaden the scope of the discussion.** Invite people to consider other possible causes of the problem: "Advertising is certainly one possible factor. What else might have contributed to a decline in sales?"

- **Get the facts.** One of the best countermoves in Scapegoat is to have facts available that support your case or point to the real reason for the problem.

The End of the Game: When Scapegoat is a group pastime, the game ends when members decide to adopt a more constructive method of problem solving. But if your boss likes to play Scapegoat, the game will only end when you get a new boss.

The Avoidance Game: "I don't want to do it, so I'm not going to do it."

To book the biggest order of her career, all Karen needed was for Gerald, the corporate attorney, to complete the sales contract. Then the customer would sign it, the deal would be final, and Karen would get a hefty commission. Although she had sent Gerald the order specifications four weeks ago, no contract was yet in sight. Karen had been down this road with Gerald before, so she wasn't completely surprised. Because this deal was a complex transaction, with several deviations from standard company policy, the CEO would have to approve the final document. Karen knew that Gerald hated discussing contracts with the CEO, who fancied himself something of a legal expert and quibbled over every clause. She had already sent Gerald three reminders and received these responses:

> First excuse: "*I can't get to it right away because I'm in the middle of an important negotiation.*"
> Second excuse: "*I was just about to start on it when the CEO gave me a rush project.*"
> Third excuse: "*I've been in meetings all week, but it's the very next thing on my list.*"

Now Gerald was completely ignoring her, so Karen wasn't sure what to do next.

Recognizing the Pattern: Avoidance is really a one-person game with unfortunate side effects for anyone who depends on the player. The game is easy to spot: the player puts off unpleasant or difficult tasks until forced to confront them. Various excuses are used as delaying tactics.

The Emotional Payoff: "I can reduce my anxiety by not thinking about an unpleasant task."

Pitfalls for Players: (1) Because they create real problems for their colleagues, Avoidance players alienate potential allies and create unnecessary adversaries; (2) when their procrastination causes critical deadlines to be missed, these players often find themselves in hot water with important people.

Exposing the Game: Exposing an Avoidance Game means talking about the player's underlying motives: "I'm beginning to think that you don't really want to deal with this, Gerald. Are you reluctant to talk to the CEO?"

Countermoves: In Avoidance, all countermoves are aimed at getting the desired results without directly attacking the player. Although an attack might temporarily make you feel better, the result is likely to be even more procrastination.

- **Never leave the timeline open-ended.** With an Avoidance player, you should always get a commitment to a specific date, even if you feel sure it will be missed. And you may want to build a delaying factor into your schedule.
- **Offer to help with the difficult part.** If you can do part of the work for the player, you may speed things up: "Gerald, how about if I draft a list of all the policy exceptions in this contract and run it by the CEO?" Although this strategy gives you more work, it also gives you more control.
- **Increase your leverage.** Sometimes you need to escalate the issue, but without appearing to threaten: "I understand that you're really busy, Gerald, but since this is such a big order, I'm going to have to let the CEO know that the final booking will be delayed."
- **Consider the power of copies.** You never want to use the CC line on your e-mails to punish people, but sometimes a well-placed copy can help to heighten the awareness of a problem. When Avoiders see that their managers or other high-leverage people know about the situation, they often get moving. But be careful if the Avoidance player is your boss; pointing out your manager's shortcomings to the higher-ups is a risky move.

The End of the Game: Avoiders never change, so you'll have to keep playing as long as they're in the picture.

SIGNS OF A TOXIC WORKPLACE

An occasional game is no big deal, but if malicious political schemes are a way of life in your office, then you need to find a healthier place to work. Sometimes one little clue can indicate a gigantic problem. Shortly after starting a new management job in an unfamiliar organization, I asked one of my staff members about a minor issue that my boss had mentioned.

"I can explain that," he said quickly. "I have a note about it in my file."

"Your file?" I asked, puzzled.

"Oh, yes, I keep records of everything I do," he replied. "It's the only way to be safe around here." I must have looked at him rather strangely, because he added, "You'll see what I mean before long."

I decided that this young man, who had previously seemed quite sensible, must have slightly paranoid tendencies. Six months later, when I started my own documentation file, his meaning had become all too clear.

Working in a toxic organization can be like living in an abusive home. Targets of abuse often have a warped view of reality, believing that they are the problem, not the abuser. I'll never forget one woman I saw in counseling whose husband not only hit her, but also left town without warning every so often and had all the utilities turned off while he was gone. After describing the situation, this poised, attractive, intelligent woman said with all seriousness, "Is that normal?" She had been in a sick relationship so long that, as far as she knew, this might just be how a marriage worked. The same thing can happen to people who spend too much time in a toxic company. If you spot a few of these danger signs, it's time to buy a new suit for job interviews.

- Power struggles and power plays are common and ongoing.
- Management egos need to be stroked on a regular basis.
- Executives are primarily focused on increasing their power or fattening their purses.
- People only talk to their managers if they absolutely have to.
- Entire departments are at war with each other.
- Management pays more attention to what employees do wrong than what they do right.
- Employees spend a lot of energy on CYA activities.

- Problems automatically trigger the search for a scapegoat.
- Gossip, put-downs, blaming, and backbiting are common among co-workers.
- Disagreements get personal and insulting.
- Co-workers have a "my way or the highway" attitude and seldom help one another.
- Unreasonably long work hours are a way of life.
- No consideration is given to personal or family issues.

Clues to toxicity sometimes show up in unusual ways. Some years ago, I recall walking into a conference room to find three of my fellow managers discussing the relative merits of different brands of antacids. "Time to leave this company," I thought. And before too long, I did.

Toxic organizations are usually the product of toxic leadership. For better or worse, the values and beliefs of top executives determine the culture of their companies. So if you find yourself in one of these unhealthy places, you have two choices: either take stress management classes and pray for a leadership change, or get out! As soon as you leave, everything happening in that sick little world will become totally irrelevant to your life.

Personal Politics

What Games Are Played in Your Workplace?

Assessing your situation:

- Check any of the games that are played by the people with whom you work.

  - ☐ The Suck-Up Game
  - ☐ The Control Game
  - ☐ The Shunning Game
  - ☐ The Superiority Game
  - ☐ The Put-Down Game
  - ☐ The In-Group Game
  - ☐ The Scapegoat Game
  - ☐ The Avoidance Game

- Do you actively participate in any of these games yourself? If so, what do you find rewarding about playing the game? What is your emotional payoff? If you're not a player, are the games interfering with your work in any way? Or making the workplace less pleasant for everyone?

Moving from assessment to action:

- If you are a game player, what change in your behavior would stop the game? Would stopping the game improve your chances of accomplishing important goals? Would it make life more pleasant for yourself and others?
- If you are an observer or target of the game, is there anything you could do to break up the game and get everyone back on a more productive course?

Are You in a Toxic Organization?

Assessing your situation:

- Do you suspect that you might be in a toxic organization? See if any of these clues apply to your situation.

  ☐ Power struggles
  ☐ Huge management egos
  ☐ Unethical management
  ☐ Warring departments
  ☐ Abusive managers
  ☐ Pervasive CYA activities
  ☐ Constantly squabbling co-workers
  ☐ Blaming and personal attacks
  ☐ Everyone out for themselves
  ☐ Ridiculously long work hours
  ☐ No concern for family needs
  ☐ Constant intolerable stress

Moving from assessment to action:

- If you have found serious signs of toxicity in your workplace, there is only one question to consider: How do you get out of there? Identify the first step in your job search and take it now!

Chapter 6

How to Commit Political Suicide

Rhonda phoned one Friday afternoon, sounding rather agitated. "I've got this new employee, Travis, who's driving me crazy," she said. "The guy's not doing a bad job, but he's so demanding and difficult! There just isn't time for all this drama right now. I've got to do something about him." I had never met Travis but, given Rhonda's description, his future didn't sound too bright. If you want to commit political suicide, simply start engaging in any behavior that consumes a disproportionate share of management's time and attention. Managers have limited tolerance for anyone who becomes an energy drain. Before long, you will be viewed as **The Problem**. And becoming The Problem is the kiss of death.

THE DANGER OF BECOMING "THE PROBLEM"

Sociologists and marketers describe a phenomenon known as the **tipping point**. A tipping point occurs when, for example, a disease unexpectedly begins to spread like wildfire, becoming an epidemic, or a new product suddenly catches on all over the country, quickly selling out in every store. Tipping points are also reached in troubled marriages: after accumulated stress and unhappiness, a particular event may "tip" one partner into seriously contemplating divorce. I often witness this "tipping" phenomenon when managers are grappling with difficult employee situations. The decision to demote or fire someone is seldom made suddenly. But the point at which such drastic action becomes an option—the tipping point—is when the person begins to be seen as The Problem. Once someone is tagged with that label, a marked shift occurs in the manager's thinking: instead of considering how to either coach or cope with the employee, the manager is now starting to fantasize about how pleasant life would be if this bothersome person were gone, and to wonder how many "last chances" should be provided before the ax falls.

When Rhonda called, I could tell that her thinking about Travis had already tipped. He was consuming entirely too much of her energy and distracting her attention from more productive activities. She was now trying to decide whether my services should be offered as one of his last chances. To understand how Travis became The Problem, let's review some highlights from his first three months on the job.

- On his first day of work, Travis tells Rhonda that human resources misrepresented the job to him. He complains about the benefits and insurance premiums.
- On his third day, for no obvious reason, Travis announces to Rhonda, "You know, I'm a pretty high-maintenance person. I really need a lot of attention." He does not appear to be joking.
- After a couple of weeks, Travis complains that the workload is heavier than he anticipated, his stomach is in knots all the time, and he hates coming to work. Yet he can't seem to describe any specific issues that Rhonda might address to improve the situation.

- Travis frequently complains that Rhonda does not seem pleased with his work. "When you act the way you do, I don't know what to think," he says, but never explains what that means. In reality, Rhonda has actually been quite happy with the quality of his work.
- Shortly before Rhonda's phone call to me, Travis asks to meet with her. "I think we need to talk," he says. "I know that we're both unhappy with this situation." But he becomes highly anxious when Rhonda suggests that perhaps he is in the wrong job.

The opposite of Political Intelligence is political idiocy. Travis might as well be waving a large warning flag that says, "I'm going to be trouble!" He seems completely clueless about how his new boss may react to this behavior, and he is certainly misreading the leverage equation. As a brand-new employee, Travis has no leverage whatsoever. He's had no time to build political capital or develop allies, and he can easily be dismissed at the end of his initial three-month probationary period. Which is exactly what happened.

Once people arrive at a conclusion, they unconsciously continue to gather evidence that supports their opinion. If you decide to back a particular political candidate, you will naturally begin to focus on the good things about her and the bad things about her opponent. After concluding that your marriage is headed for divorce court, you are much less likely to see your spouse's virtues and much more likely to notice his flaws. Conversely, couples in the initial throes of true love see only the signs that they are meant for each other and ignore any omen of future difficulties. Once an employee has tipped into The Problem category, managers are automatically primed to notice any behavior that confirms this conclusion. The bottom line here is that being labeled The Problem puts you in a very deep hole, and digging yourself out can be tough.

Most people don't wake up each morning thinking, "Now what could I do to wreck my career today?" No sane person wants to become The Problem, yet many people rush headlong down the path to political suicide. Some are victims of their own chronic, self-destructive habits. Others simply make bad choices about how to act in difficult situations. There are four common causes of career destruction: (1) poorly controlled emotions; (2) a victim mentality; (3) self-centered goals; and (4) foolish reactions to change.

THE HAZARDS OF UNCONTROLLED EMOTION

Most business offices are fairly calm, orderly, rational places—at least on the surface. Beneath that placid facade, however, lies a hotbed of emotion. All workers have the same feelings on the job that they experience in every other aspect of their lives. They've just learned not to show them, which is actually a darned good thing; if people demonstrated their true feelings all the time, little would be accomplished and few colleagues would be speaking to each other. One guaranteed way to become The Problem is to let your emotions run amok on the job.

- Brandon worked for a retail store owner who was slow to take action and often tried to skirt difficult issues. As Brandon's frustration with this behavior grew, he began storming into the owner's office and yelling till he became red in the face. The owner, who had previously considered making Brandon a partner, decided that perhaps that wasn't such a good plan after all. Brandon never knew about the opportunity that he had unwittingly thrown away.

- Lois, a department manager, was completely intimidated by her employees. If they criticized her decisions or complained about her management style, Lois meekly listened without responding. When problems arose with her employees' work, she was so fearful of their reaction that she never mentioned the issues to them. Eventually, her boss concluded that Lois wasn't management material and replaced her with a stronger person.

The two emotions that most frequently lead people down the road to ruin are anger and anxiety. Everyone feels angry or anxious at work from time to time. That's perfectly normal. But problems arise if persistent negative feelings create a pattern of destructive behavior that interferes with your results or relationships. Your emotions are completely private unless your behavior telegraphs the message to everyone around you.

Anger is the most serious problem, because too much hostility causes people to walk the other way when they see you coming. Angry people intimidate others and are simply not pleasant to be around. Dangerous behavior patterns that arise from poorly controlled anger include complaining, rebellion, and confrontation:

- **Complaining:** Tom is a salesperson who constantly gripes to his colleagues about his boss, gripes to his boss about his colleagues, and gripes to upper management about what's wrong with the company.
- **Rebellion:** Carol is a social worker who resents authority. She disagrees with her manager's decisions, refuses to obey policies that she doesn't like, and encourages her clients to bend the rules.
- **Confrontation:** Ray is a manager who frequently yells and curses at his staff, berating them for making mistakes and ridiculing any new ideas they suggest. He has been known to literally bring people to tears in meetings.

When these anger-based behaviors become too pervasive, the offenders begin to be viewed as more of a hindrance than a help. And at that point, they are just one short step from the exit.

At the other extreme, overly anxious behavior sends the message that you are weak, worried, and dependent. Unless being a doormat is part of your job description, insecurity is not usually a career asset. Anxious people self-destruct because they either fail to address difficult issues or appear to be totally dispensable. Timidity, neediness, and hiding are some of the troublesome behavior patterns in this category.

- **Timidity:** Bob is an experienced engineer who is afraid to speak up in department meetings for fear that he may say something stupid. As a result, he sits quietly during discussions and seldom expresses an opinion. When faced with any disagreement, he capitulates quickly just to keep the peace.
- **Neediness:** Because Anne constantly worries that her work may not be good enough, she needs frequent reassurance that everything is okay. At each step of a project, she checks with her boss to be sure she's on the right track. She can be brought to tears by any negative feedback or critical comments.
- **Hiding:** Dennis is a computer programmer who is uncomfortable around people. He prefers to work alone in his cubicle. If he sees an executive coming down the hall, he may duck into the restroom to avoid a conversation. Some of his colleagues don't know Dennis's name and many have no idea what he does.

Having angry or anxious feelings is part of being human, but allowing them to control your behavior is politically disastrous. Succumbing to your emotions is like drinking too much: in the short run, an occasional binge may do little harm and make you feel better, but chronic abuse will inevitably lead to long-term problems.

While we're on this topic, a word should be said about one more emotion: lust. Some unknown wag once coined this sensible saying: "Don't look for your honey where you get your money." Politically astute folks direct their desires, fantasies, and romantic overtures away from work colleagues. Most workplace romances eventually die out, leaving a trail of political debris in their wake. If you think you've found the one, true love of your life at the office, then you may want to take the chance. But weigh the risks carefully before you proceed.

Regardless of whether the emotional issue is anger, anxiety, or lust, those who lack self-control will inevitably enter the Dimwit

category sooner or later. And since Dimwits are destined to become The Problem, that is a risky place to be.

SEEING YOURSELF AS THE VICTIM

People talk to themselves all the time. As you go through the day,
your mind automatically produces a running internal commen-
tary about the events you experience and the people you encounter.
You may sit quietly and smile while your boss critiques your project proposal, but an entirely different conversation is going on in
your head: "This guy is really an idiot. He obviously doesn't understand the project. In fact, he never takes the time to really understand anything. I don't know why I stay in this job anyway. I
think I'll polish up my résumé." Is this hypocritical? Heck, no.
Masking our internal reactions is an important skill in both office
politics and everyday life. No one wants to know what everyone
else is thinking. But here's the problem: you have to be careful
about what you tell yourself, because people tend to believe their
own messages. If you fall into the habit of thinking "This guy is
an idiot" every time your boss speaks, you will automatically begin
looking for supportive evidence. "My boss is an idiot" will soon
become an entrenched belief and eventually creep into your communication patterns. Before too long, your boss will start to get
the message that you think he's not too bright—and that realization will change the way that he talks to himself about you! Possibly leading to undesirable consequences. You must always be
mindful of what psychologists call "self-talk," because what you
say to yourself shapes your attitudes and your behavior.

Have you ever found thoughts like these going through your
mind: "No one appreciates all the work I do around here"; "They
just don't want to pay me what I'm worth"; "I always get passed
over for the really good assignments." Occasionally throwing
yourself a small pity party is a harmless indulgence, but if you
have such thoughts on a daily basis, watch out! You may be creating a **Victim Identity**—one of the most politically destructive

forms of self-talk. For some, mild paranoia just seems to be a natural state of mind. Put them in any job and they will find an enemy somewhere. Other victims start out as self-sacrificing Martyrs who go to great lengths to please others, then become resentful when their efforts fail to be fully appreciated. Sometimes a victim mentality is triggered by some "unfair" event that suddenly casts the world in a different light. All subsequent actions and interactions are then carefully screened for signs of unfair treatment—and, as always, when evidence is sought, it becomes easy to find. The aggrieved party soon accumulates a truckload of "proof" that her conclusion was correct: she is indeed a victim. Since every victim must have at least one persecutor, anyone assuming a Victim Identity will automatically identify certain managers or co-workers as adversaries, then begin to treat them accordingly. Thus begins a vicious cycle that can lead to political suicide.

Dorothy, a supervisor in a government agency, applied for promotion to section head, but the job was given to another candidate. As she pondered this rejection, Dorothy was puzzled. She had the required experience for the position, she always received excellent appraisals, managers frequently praised her work, her unit was performing above expectations . . . so why didn't she get the job? She finally concluded that her manager had probably failed to support her for the promotion. Considering this possibility, Dorothy recalled the times that her boss had left her out of meetings or rejected her ideas—"Yes," she decided, "he clearly must not have a very high opinion of me. Otherwise, I surely would have gotten that job." So Dorothy began to cast herself as the victim, with her boss in the role of adversary. As her resentment grew, Dorothy stopped asking her manager for advice or dropping by his office for friendly chats. Then she began to notice that he no longer sought her opinion and spent less time with her than with the other supervisors. She gradually developed the habit of communicating with him primarily through e-mail. When her next performance appraisal included some negative comments, Dorothy filed a grievance with human resources. After these charges were deemed to be invalid, she began to gripe about her unfair treatment to anyone who would listen. When she applied for another promotion and was again rejected, she wrote a scathing letter to the department head complaining about her boss. At this point, sadly, Dorothy crossed the tipping point and became The Problem. She may keep her job, but she will never, ever be promoted. This may or may not be "fair"—but it's a fact.

Dorothy was not torpedoed by her boss, but by her own negative self-talk. Suppose that, instead of assuming a Victim Identity, Dorothy had put aside her thoughts of unfairness, met with her boss, and said, "I was very disappointed about not getting the promotion to section head. I'd really like to know what I could do to improve my chances next time." Perhaps she could have saved her career. So be careful about what you say to yourself. If "poor little me" is a recurrent theme in your internal (or external) conversations, you need to change your negative self-talk before you develop a victim mentality.

What if you really *are* a victim, though? If you are facing true discrimination because of your race or age or some other illegal consideration, that gets a bit tougher, because you have some choices to make. First, be sure that your assessment is correct. Sometimes illegal treatment is easy to spot: I once knew an African-American gentleman who found a noose hanging in his work locker. Not much question about that situation. But consider this one: a young black woman who shared a secretary with her white boss complained that the secretary always did the boss's work first. She attributed this situation to racial prejudice, but odds are that the secretary, knowing who would determine her next raise, had made a political choice, not a racial one. Fortunately, the young woman decided to talk the situation over with her HR manager, who was able to help her view it differently.

A person's true motives can be difficult to determine. If, however, you believe that you are indeed experiencing illegal discrimination, you have reached a fork in the road: Do you quietly try to overcome these prejudicial attitudes or do you file an official complaint? The gentleman who found the noose certainly needed to let someone know, but the best approach is less clear if you fail to receive a promotion or get a negative performance review. In a perfect world, you could make your protest, have the problem investigated, and go on to a successful and prejudice-free career. But I have to give you some unwelcome news. In the unjust and unreasonable real world, once you file an official grievance, you have crossed over an invisible line and become an adversary to management. No one will tell you this; no one will begin to treat you differently, at least if they have any sense. Yet I can guarantee that managers will be having hushed conversations about you and viewing you as a potential problem. Let me be quite clear: I am *not* suggesting that people should tolerate illegal treatment. I applaud those who are brave enough to take a stand against prejudice. When you consider going public with such a charge, though, you need to be aware of the political ramifications of that decision. Often the best course of action is to consult a trusted friend or colleague to get another perspective and discuss possible strategies. If you have a helpful HR department, you may find that they can provide good advice. Should you conclude that getting a fair shake is impossible, however, your best option may be to find a more enlightened place to work.

WHEN IT'S ALL ABOUT YOU

Selfishness is another contributor to political downfall. All Sociopaths have this problem. They just want what they want when they want it, with no regard for the common good—like basketball players who always take the shot and never pass off to their teammates. Sociopathic people can be found at all levels. One of my clients has an administrative assistant who feels that the job is beneath her. She will happily tackle any task that she views as "professional," but routinely ignores mundane activities like copying, filing, and answering the phone. Why doesn't she simply change jobs? I have no idea, but I don't predict a long future for her in this one. At the other end of the organizational ladder, you find self-centered CEOs, like Dave. Here are a few examples of the behavior that qualifies Dave for this category:

- After being summoned to corporate headquarters for a meeting with Dave, seven executives spend the entire day sitting and waiting in the lobby while he does other things.
- One Halloween night, Dave wants to talk to a manager about a matter that could easily wait until the next day. Dave tracks him down, finds him out trick-or-treating with his young daughter, and orders him to take her home and come into the office immediately.
- Dave's company is located in a Southern city that only sees significant snow about once every five years. After one of these rare snowstorms hits, Dave orders the facilities manager to purchase a Jeep with a snowplow attachment so that no one will ever again miss one of his meetings because of weather.

I could go on, but you get the idea. Let me ask you to predict Dave's behavior in this situation: It's Saturday evening. Dave wants to talk to an important customer about a large order. Dave calls the customer at home and is told by his wife that they are in the middle of their daughter's sixteenth birthday party. So what does Dave do? That's right—he insists that the reluctant customer come to the phone and discuss the order. The following week, the customer calls a board member to complain. Now that you've gotten to know Dave, are you surprised that he was eventually fired? Even a CEO can become The Problem.

Not all self-centered people are Sociopaths, however. Some are Martyrs, acting in the interest of what they believe to be a higher cause. And dedication to that cause takes precedence over all other considerations. Single-minded advocacy is great if you're a lobbyist but, in most business situations, overzealousness is politically imprudent. Being so narrowly focused, these advocates lack the sense of balance required for political success. After making a change to the petty cash policy, the new executive director of a nonprofit group found herself faced with a crusading finance manager. Although the executive director was doing nothing illegal or immoral, her new petty cash policy so infuriated the finance manager that he refused to sign off on purchases, and sent a letter of complaint to the board. Although he finally backed off, the finance manager almost sacrificed his job for the sake of petty differences over petty cash. Many professional people struggle with the balance between professional standards and organizational realities. Nurses have to fit many patients into a crowded schedule, engineers have limited time to create a workable product design, marketers can't afford the ideal advertising campaign, lawyers have to defend their bosses' risky decisions. For professionals, the ability to successfully walk this tightrope is a critical ingredient of Political Intelligence.

Winners are able to view a situation from various points of view, but Sociopaths and cause-driven Martyrs see everything through the lens of their own desires, finding it difficult to shift their thinking to a different perspective. Extreme selfishness and misguided advocacy often lead to political self-destruction, because no organization can succeed if its members act only in their own self-interest.

FOOLISH REACTIONS TO CHANGE

For some previously successful people, their political decline and fall is triggered by a particularly stressful change. Suddenly their boss, job, or organization is no longer compatible with their belief about how work "should" be done. Such a change can occur in many ways:

- Debbie, a creative, free-spirited graphic designer, left her job with a small ad agency to join the marketing department of a large corporation.

- Jack, a successful retail salesperson, was asked to take a newly created management position when increased business led to an expansion of the sales staff.
- Anita, a manager in a government agency, found herself reporting to a new department head after an election brought a different political party to power.
- Rick, a software engineer, discovered that job expectations had changed when his small technology company was acquired by a larger competitor.

Sometimes we choose a change, as Debbie and Jack did when they accepted new positions. Other changes are thrust upon us by resignations, mergers, or reorganizations. But regardless of the cause, people who lack Political Intelligence may quickly decide that the new state of affairs is "wrong." Then they reinforce this feeling with negative self-talk: "This company is totally disorganized." "That woman just doesn't understand how we do things around here." "These managers don't want to take time to do things the right way." "Nobody cares about the employees anymore." Because "they're wrong" automatically implies "I'm right," this politically suicidal reaction often marks the beginning of an adversarial relationship, which, left unchecked, can easily escalate into a power struggle. We all know how those turn out: the person with the least leverage loses.

Life, as we have already established, is not fair. When circumstances change, things sometimes just don't go your way. This is not usually a matter of right versus wrong, however, but simply a case of something being different. Your new boss will probably have different habits and expectations than your old boss. That doesn't mean she's wrong. When you change jobs, your new employer will probably have different policies and procedures. That doesn't mean they're wrong. If your business is acquired by another company, the culture will probably be somewhat different. That doesn't make it wrong. Unless their actions are illegal or unethical, new people are not bad or evil or mistaken; they're just not what you are accustomed to. So you have three options: you can either (1) adapt to the new way; (2) leave for greener pastures; or (3) become a pain in the ass and eventually be deemed The Problem. The choice is yours.

The four people mentioned above made choices that illustrate how differently these situations can turn out.

- Debbie got into a visible and vocal power struggle with her new boss, making no secret of her belief that the cold and bureaucratic corporate environment stifled creativity and rewarded mediocre work. After nine months, Debbie's manager got tired of arguing and let her go. Fighting the organizational culture is a pointless battle unless you're the CEO (and sometimes even then). You're not going to change it.

- Jack quickly became frustrated in his new management job. He and the store owner, who had previously had a pleasant working relationship, began to get into shouting matches over policies and procedures. Fortunately, Jack finally recognized that the problem was not the owner, but his own adjustment to a management role, and they were able to work out their differences.

- Anita immediately disliked her new boss, whom she viewed as a political hack with little concern for the agency's mission. She expressed her unhappiness by aggressively debating him in staff meetings and ignoring projects that he viewed as high priority. He, in turn, began to override her decisions. Realizing that she would probably never be happy in this new environment, Anita chose to leave for another opportunity.

- Rick, despite his initial dismay, eventually found that his job became more interesting after the acquisition, because being part of a larger company provided a wider variety of technical challenges. He continued to work there quite happily.

Of the four, Debbie was the only one who opted for political self-destruction. The others made wiser decisions.

WARNING SIGNS OF POLITICAL TROUBLE

Many political suicides are so caught up in their own concerns or delusions that when the ax falls, they are totally shocked. Others sense that they are in political danger, but haven't the foggiest idea how to fix the situation. For the clueless group, the warning signs of political trouble are listed below, in order of severity. If you spot any of these signals, you have a problem that needs to be addressed. And it needs to be addressed quickly.

Level 1: Something is not quite right.

- You have been experiencing a growing uneasiness, with frequent angry thoughts about unfairness. (Sometimes people feel like a victim because they are actually about to become one.)
- You find yourself alone a lot. No one stops by your desk unless they have a specific purpose. You don't get invited to lunch, weddings, baby showers, golf outings, baseball nights, and so on. You seem to have become a social outcast.
- Your boss ignores you, fails to notify you of meetings, neglects to give you information, or makes pointed remarks indicating that you are requiring too much time and attention.
- Your boss has a Serious Talk with you about some aspect of your performance or your personality. If your manager tends to be a little wimpy, this talk may sound more like a chat than a reprimand. Consider your manager's style—anything out of the ordinary counts as a warning.
- A personal coach is hired to help you. The bad news is that you are seen as having some "issues" that need to be ad-

dressed. The good news is that someone is still willing to invest in your future success. Executives seldom spend money on people they consider hopeless.

Level 2: The future looks questionable.

- An important assignment that would logically be yours is given to someone else. If that someone else has designs on your job or is a rival for your next promotion, this is a troubling development.
- You are turned down for promotions more than once. The first time, they may have just found a better applicant. But, more than that, you're starting to see a pattern. And it's not good.
- After acquiring a new boss, your leverage seems to be slipping away. You are not consulted as frequently, given as much information, or included in as many meetings as before. If you don't take some action, you are probably headed for that Serious Talk.
- Someone from human resources initiates the Serious Talk. This is an indication that management people have been thinking unkindly about you for some time. You may already be considered The Problem.

Level 3: A sudden career change may lie ahead.

- Following a reorganization, you find that you have suffered a reduction in staff, title, responsibilities, or reporting level; or you've been physically shuffled off to the hinterlands. You were probably given some lame excuse for this change. If believing it makes you feel better, go ahead—but recognize that any kind of reduction is a bad sign.
- Your boss's boss gets into the act, reinforcing a Serious Talk that you have already had with someone else. This is not just a warning signal. It's a huge flashing neon sign

that says you're about to become roadkill on the corporate highway.

- Rumors of layoffs are going around and people are starting to avoid you or look at you sadly. If these are human resources people, start working on your résumé.

Unless you're prone to paranoid delusions, these warning signs clearly indicate that something undesirable is going on. To start addressing the issue, you need to determine whether the trouble originates with you or with your environment. Here's the Catch-22: the difficulty may be due, in part, to your inability to see the situation clearly—and if you can't see things clearly, it's hard to accurately determine the cause of the problem.

Social psychologists describe a common distortion in human thinking called **attribution error,** which is shorthand for, "It's a heckuva lot easier to blame somebody else." A simple example should easily demonstrate our propensity for attribution errors. Suppose you get a promotion or a big raise. Why did you receive this reward? Because of your superior abilities and performance, of course. But suppose you get turned down for the promotion—why did that happen? Probably because the interview process wasn't fair, or because the person who got it has been sucking up for years, or because management doesn't understand what's really needed in that job. Or something, anything, other than your own possible shortcomings. These self-serving attributions bolster our egos: when something good happens to us, we credit this fortunate outcome to some positive personal characteristic—but when bad things happen, we look outside ourselves for the cause. If you feel that you have become a political target, self-serving attributions can seem like your best friend because they're so comforting: all this pain and suffering is certainly not *your* fault. But if you really are contributing to your own downfall, such mental thumb-sucking just keeps you from correcting your destructive behaviors, habits, or attitudes. They will inevitably come back to haunt you in the future.

To avoid attribution errors, you need to strive for objectivity and look for patterns. Say, for example, that you have decided your boss is an unreasonable jerk. Do others share your opinion? Is she an unreasonable jerk with everyone or just with you? And what about you—have you felt that many of your managers were unreasonable, or just this one? If your boss has difficulties with several staff members, then the problem may very well lie with her. But if you have a history of dissatisfaction with bosses, then you may need to look in the mirror. If neither one of you seems to have a problematic pattern, the difficulty may lie in the combination of your individual work styles. Some personality types just don't mesh very well.

When political warning signals start to flash, examine the patterns in the situation. First, take a good look at what's going on around you. If everyone is working till midnight, keeping a CYA file, or worried about recording devices in the conference room, then you're in a toxic workplace. Over time, remaining in a sick environment will either completely undermine your self-confidence or warp you so thoroughly that you will be unfit for normal employment. Forget political strategy and exit as quickly as possible. On the other hand, if your colleagues are happily and productively engaged while you're fuming with rage, then you need to take a closer look at yourself. Review your work history, relationships, and reactions to authority, and look for any common themes. Have you been laid off or fired more than once? Have you been repeatedly turned down for promotions or important assignments? Have you frequently thought that you were misunderstood or being treated unfairly? Have you often felt angry toward colleagues or found them annoying? When talking to managers, do you become argumentative or defensive, or do managers tend to scare you? If you are a manager, do you often become angry or annoyed with employees? Have people complained about your management style? Such honest self-scrutiny is not easy, because our brains seem to automatically dredge up all the possible reasons to blame someone else. Recognizing the destructive patterns in your own behavior is the single most important step in averting political suicide. Once you've identified them, you need to immediately begin corrective action.

POLITICAL PLASTIC SURGERY

Forestalling career annihilation may not be easy, but it is possible. If you sense that you have become The Problem, then you need a political makeover—that is, your image must be quickly and drastically restructured. Consider the plight of Randall, a manager on the brink of being demoted. The high turnover rate in Randall's district office had attracted the attention of his boss, who was becoming extremely concerned. Based on conversations and observations, she concluded that Randall was the cause of this turnover problem. She was right. Randall closely monitored his employees, obsessed about irrelevant details, got involved in the smallest decisions, and offered criticism much more frequently than praise. He was a classic micromanager whose behavior created serious morale problems. To save himself, Randall had to change. But altering ingrained habits is not nearly as simple as people think.

The acronym AMISH sums up the five steps required to accomplish any personal behavior change: Awareness, Motivation, Identification, Substitution, and Habit Replacement. Even though this process has nothing to do with religious communities in Pennsylvania, perhaps the label will help you remember the steps.

- **Awareness:** If you don't know that a problem exists, how can you change? Without feedback to the contrary, most of us believe that we're doing just fine. Many managers drop subtle hints about their concerns, so you need to be alert. "Seems like a lot of your salespeople have left for other jobs this year," Randall's boss might say. A politically obtuse Randall would reply, "Yeah, the company just doesn't pay these people enough. You need to look into that." But a politically intelligent Randall, recognizing this comment as a tiny little warning sign, would say, "I've been concerned about that, too. Do you think that our district office is different from the others somehow?" When you sense political trouble, you must find out what people are thinking, even if it's painful. Unfortunately, some bosses practice "psychic management": they think and think and think about an employee problem, but never share their thoughts with the offending party—thereby allowing the poor soul to become The Problem without ever being told. If your manager never comments on your job performance, soliciting feedback occasionally is a good idea.

- **Motivation:** The fact that someone else has issues with your behavior doesn't necessarily mean that you agree. If you don't think you have a problem, you certainly won't be motivated to change anything. Randall never saw himself as a micromanager. From his point of view, he was thorough and careful and concerned about quality. Can you see an attribution error developing here? But Randall will never resurrect himself politically if he maintains this denial. When someone indicates that your behavior is a problem, don't automatically reject that possibility. Instead, try to understand how your actions may be affecting other people. Then perhaps you will be motivated to try some new approaches.

- **Identification:** Even if Randall comes to accept that he is indeed a micromanager, he still must identify exactly which behaviors need to change. His "micromanagement" must therefore be defined in terms of specific actions: Which documents should he stop reviewing? What decisions can he delegate? Which details should he just let go? If your problem behavior has been described in broad, fuzzy terms—like "bad attitude" or "poor communication" or "lack of initiative"—you need to get more specifics. Then you can decide what you need to do differently.

- **Substitution:** Stopping one behavior automatically implies that you will replace it with another. If you stop speeding, you will start driving more slowly. If you stop yelling, you will start speaking more softly. In fact, any behavior change has a greater chance of success when you define it in positive terms instead of negative ones. Saying, "I have to stop getting angry" doesn't tell you what to do instead.

But saying, "When I feel angry in meetings, I'm going to take deep breaths and speak calmly" will give you a positive goal. If you want to eliminate a troublesome behavior, you have to decide what helpful behavior to substitute. When Randall feels the urge to scrutinize the draft of a sales brochure with a magnifying glass, what will he do instead? Perhaps he could decide to compliment the designer on all the positive features and only red-pencil major concerns. Or he might decide to delegate brochure review to a lower-level manager. Always remember that you are capable of making conscious decisions about your behavior. To rehabilitate yourself politically, you must quickly learn to make wiser choices.

- **Habit Replacement:** A successful political makeover means that new habits have been developed. You have permanently adopted more effective ways of acting and interacting. But old habits don't vanish overnight, so expect a few relapses. No doubt Randall will occasionally become too involved in small decisions or overzealous in editing a document. If he persists in his efforts to act differently, however, his new habits will eventually begin to operate on automatic pilot.

When you are trying to recast your image, remember that others will not immediately notice the change in your behavior. If you're waiting for the applause, it may seem awfully quiet for a while. Even if Randall completely alters his management style tomorrow, people won't detect the change immediately. Once they do, they still won't believe that it's going to "stick" until evidence accumulates over time. So when you are trying to change, be patient. Don't expect instant acclaim for the new you.

But, you may ask, what if I don't need a makeover? What if I'm really not a problem and other people just take things the wrong way? Well, then you need to learn to do those "things" differently. Because if you're not a problem, but people think you are, the political effect is unfortunately the same. One of my coaching clients, Tracy, was told by his boss that he had a negative attitude and was resistant to change. This completely puzzled Tracy, who insisted that he truly loved his job and had willingly implemented every change his boss proposed. Upon closer examination of his communication style, however, the source of this misperception became clear. Tracy has a real gift for seeing the flaws, risks, and hazards in any idea or proposal, which is a good talent to have. But Tracy exercised this ability a bit too quickly in conversations with his boss. Every time his manager proposed a new idea, Tracy immediately pointed out the possible problems. Tracy felt that he was being helpful, but his boss understandably interpreted these criticisms as "a negative attitude and resistance to change." To avoid political trouble, Tracy needed to change this communication pattern even though he was doing nothing "wrong." So he decided to develop a new habit: looking for—and mentioning—the positive aspects of an idea before describing the potential pitfalls. Problem solved.

Regardless of whether political reconstruction requires major surgery or only involves a minor adjustment, we tend to resist it. Listening to criticism, admitting flaws, and changing habits isn't anyone's idea of fun. But the result of ignoring obvious warning signs is almost always political suicide.

Personal Politics

Are You a Candidate for Political Suicide?

Assessing your situation:

- Think honestly about your situation at work and answer the questions below.

Do you frequently feel angry or anxious at work?	YES	NO	MAYBE
If so, is your anger or anxiety obvious to other people?	YES	NO	MAYBE
Do you feel that you have been treated very unfairly at work?	YES	NO	MAYBE
Do you mentally review this unfair treatment on a regular basis?	YES	NO	MAYBE
Do you frequently talk about your unfair treatment with people at work?	YES	NO	MAYBE
Are you having recurrent lustful fantasies about someone at work?	YES	NO	MAYBE
Are you involved in a romantic or sexual relationship at work?	YES	NO	MAYBE

Do you focus exclusively on your own goals, with little thought for others?	YES	NO	MAYBE
Would co-workers describe you as difficult to work with?	YES	NO	MAYBE
Have you felt resentful about a recent change at work?	YES	NO	MAYBE
Has this resentment caused you to exhibit annoying or disruptive behavior?	YES	NO	MAYBE
Has a manager or HR person indicated that you need to make some changes?	YES	NO	MAYBE

- If you have more than a couple of "yes" or "maybe" answers, then you could be on the verge of political problems—or you may already have them.

Moving from assessment to action:

- In any area where you checked "yes" or "maybe," you need to start adjusting your thoughts, attitudes, and actions. The fact that others may be behaving badly or treating you poorly is completely irrelevant. You need to clarify your goals, focus on the future, and concentrate on things that are within your control. Start by deciding if your current job is right for you. If not, what is your first step toward leaving? If so, what can you do to improve the situation?

Do You Need Political Plastic Surgery?

Assessing your situation:

- If you have become your own greatest obstacle to success, then you need to start your political makeover. Take a good look at your own behavior. What is causing others to conclude that you are a problem? What behaviors do you need to stop? What new behaviors do you need to adopt? Fill out the AMISH chart below.

Awareness	Motivation	Identification	Substitution	Habits
What am I doing that is creating a problem?	Why is it important for me to change?	What are the specific harmful behaviors that I need to stop?	If I stop this behavior, what helpful behavior will I put in its place?	How will I know when my new behavior has become a habit?

Moving from assessment to action:

- Now that you have defined your desired behavior, identify the situations in which you need to use it. Anticipate the people or events that are most likely to trigger your old, unproductive actions. Mentally rehearse how you will handle those difficult situations. Visualize success!

- Determine whether you need to have any discussions to start repairing perceptions. Do you need to tell anyone about your intention to change? If people from management or HR have had a serious talk with you, then you should definitely follow up with them, especially if you were initially unreceptive to their feedback. The purpose of these conversations is to declare your desire to change and describe what you plan to do differently. You must *not* get defensive, argue, complain, or blame. If you don't have this much self-control, then don't have the discussion.
- After a while, request some feedback to see how things are going. Follow-up meetings with your boss, colleagues, HR, or other relevant people will not only give you a progress assessment, but also send the message that you are motivated, open to communication, and trying to do things differently.

Chapter 7

Power, Power, Who Has the Power?

To play the political game, you have to understand power: who has it, how to get it, how to use it. Yet talking openly about power is completely prohibited. To come right out and say, "I wish I had more power," or "How much power do you have?" or "I enjoy having power over you," would be much too honest. But because power permeates the atmosphere of every organization, Winners must be able to accurately determine how that power is distributed. An army colonel, describing his recent transition into the corporate world, said, "You know, life is much simpler when the uniform tells you exactly how much power someone has. When everyone's wearing a business suit, things take a little longer to figure out." How very true. Appearances are often deceiving.

Imagine that you have just started work with a new company. On your first day, you meet many people, including Steve and Rose. Steve, the vice president of global business strategy, is wearing an expensive suit and has an impressive office in the executive suite with his own personal assistant stationed outside his door. During your brief conversation, he describes his international travels and mentions his recent golf game with the CEO. Rose, an employee relations specialist, dresses unassumingly, works in a cubicle, and does not appear to have an assistant. She warmly welcomes you to the company, asking several questions about your background and your new job. When you inquire about her role, she smiles and says, "Oh, I just handle all the little projects that no one else wants!" Rating their relative power on a 1-to-10 scale, you give an 8 to Steve and a 3 to Rose.

Over the next few weeks, you notice that whenever you pass Steve's office, he's sitting alone, working at his computer. You have yet to see him with the CEO. If you stop to say hello, he winds up telling you long, rambling stories about his past accomplishments. And while all the other executives are madly preparing for the quarterly board meeting, Steve's still just sitting there. You downgrade Steve's power rating from an 8 to a 5. Rose, on the other hand, seems to show up in many different meetings. She is on a first-name basis with all the executives and speaks frequently with the CEO's assistant. When you ask anyone about a policy or procedure, the answer often begins with, "*I think Rose probably knows about that*," or "*If you ask Rose, she can tell you what to do*." A power upgrade seems to be in order for Rose, maybe from a 3 to a 5.

Eventually you learn that, during a recent reorganization, Steve was shuffled into a meaningless job with a fancy title. He is not being discouraged from seeking employment elsewhere. Final power rating for Steve: 2. He gets a couple of points just for having an executive-level position. Rose, you discover, is a twenty-year employee who is respected and trusted by everyone. She works with people at all levels, has a broad knowledge of the company, and remains in her current job only because she has no interest in being promoted. Final power rating for Rose: 8. If you are looking for an ally, Rose is the way to go. Steve, it turns out, is just an empty suit.

POSITION POWER AND PERSONAL POWER

Both your position and your personal characteristics contribute to your power allotment. **Position power,** which comes with the job, is automatically available to any occupant of a particular role. Hierarchical authority is the most obvious example: the higher your level on the organization chart, the more decisions you get to make. If you're the senior vice president of international something-or-other, you can probably order lots of people around. And, the higher you go, the more access you have to information and resources. However, position power is not solely related to organizational level. For one thing, every organization has higher-status and lower-status jobs. In any company that has a product on the market, sales will be a high-status function. Physicians will top the pecking order in a medical center, and design engineers will be given more status in an electronics company. Why? Because these are the bet-the-business functions, without which the company cannot succeed.

But you don't have to be high-level or high-status to find sources of power in your job. Many humble positions can provide access to important people, opportunities to develop expertise, or a platform for leverage-building activities. Consider the job of receptionist. Receptionists can't tell anyone what to do, but they talk with many people, leading to the development of valuable relationships. If they put forth the effort, receptionists can use this rather low-level, low-status position to acquire business knowledge and a network of allies. If you're thinking, "That's all well and good, but receptionists still don't have any real power," then you're missing the point and confusing power with authority. True, a receptionist has little authority, but she does have access to information and connections. Another source of power, specialized knowledge, is available to those in "expert" positions, jobs which exist to provide in-depth expertise in a specific area. Greg worked in the tax department, a fairly low-profile location. But by developing extremely detailed knowledge of the tax code, Greg acquired a great deal of leverage. He was known as a veritable tax genius. Management would have felt completely helpless addressing a tax issue without Greg, giving him virtually complete job security. As the company grew and became more global, the tax department expanded and Greg eventually became a vice president. Certain other positions, because of their organizational location, provide the occupants with a unique platform. One of my clients has companywide responsibility for training in a healthcare corporation. This broad platform allows her to get involved with a variety of important projects, learn about many aspects of the business, and communicate with people from all levels and functions. She recently used her position power to organize a corporate learning and development council composed of middle managers from different departments. Working with this group will not only make her more effective, but also greatly increase her network of potential allies. The point here is that virtually every job contains some power potential—the challenge is to make the most of it.

Unfortunately, some people either fail to recognize their position power or seem to fear using it. Bert was one of those people. His position, senior consulting engineer, was given only to those who had reached the pinnacle of technical excellence, automatically conferring prestige, visibility, and the chance to mentor junior staff. Bert seldom made suggestions to his less experienced colleagues, however, because he feared they might view him as condescending or intrusive. As a result, he missed many opportunities to improve the company's products and to increase his own leverage. Even managers sometimes shy away from using position power. I know one advertising director who is quite comfortable using her power upward but not downward. She consistently makes the most of her access to upper management, getting involved in high-level projects and developing a valuable network of executive allies. But because she is reluctant to address performance issues with her staff, people sometimes question her management ability. Whenever you fail to capitalize on your position power, you automatically reduce your leverage.

Personal power derives not from your position but from your own special characteristics and abilities. We all have innate strengths that can increase our personal power. Jessica, a secretary in an office that I visit regularly, is a cheerful, outgoing person who always remembers my name and the fact that I drink tea.

Her friendliness is completely genuine—it's just part of being Jessica. Because she is a natural people magnet, Jessica has a lot more personal power than those secretaries who barely look up when someone walks in. Her warm and friendly nature automatically creates allies and will serve her well in any job she ever holds.

Andrew, a director of marketing, has a different gift. Much of his personal power comes from his obvious intelligence. A graduate of both West Point and the Harvard Business School, Andrew was an electrical engineer before embarking on a career in marketing. Among his colleagues, he is known as the person to seek out when you are trying to think strategically about a problem. However, any strength, carried too far, becomes a weakness. Andrew is so bright and so serious that he can sometimes make people uncomfortable. As he described it, "I really don't like nonsensical banter that is not edifying"—which clearly illustrates that Andrew could benefit from learning to lighten up a bit. Increasing your personal power means not only using your strengths, but also reducing your weakness.

As we saw with Steve and Rose, evaluating someone's political power is not always simple. Even in the Army, where everyone is labeled, one three-star general is not necessarily the political equal of another. Here are some questions to consider in determining a person's power level:

- Do top managers know who they are?
- Could the CEO find their office without a map?
- Do they talk more about the past or the future?
- Is their body language confident or submissive?
- Do people listen when they speak?
- Do people trust them with information?
- What meetings do they attend?
- How many people know who they are?
- With whom do they have lunch?
- What email distribution lists are they on?
- Who can they go to see without an appointment?
- When they want something, do they get it?

Being able to accurately assess the distribution of power is a fundamental aspect of Political Intelligence, one which can help you safely navigate political minefields and avoid political pitfalls. These power clues may be helpful:

People with HIGH power...	People with LOW power...
• Are inluded in important decisions • Are well-regarded by people at all levels • Communicate with people in high-level positions • Have information or skills that are valued by others • Are trusted with confidential information • Are involved in important projects • Have expertise that is hard to replace	• May not be doing important work • May talk a lot about the past • May try to sound more important than they are • May drop names of important people • May like to spend most of their time alone • May have little interest in their work • May avoid conflict or handle it poorly

AVOIDING FOOLISH POWER MISTAKES

When it comes to using power, people make a lot of mistakes. Some timid souls, fearing that they will be perceived as pushy, overbearing, or insensitive, simply give their power away—often empowering obnoxious colleagues who actually are pushy, over-bearing, and insensitive. At the other extreme are the egomaniacs who try to look as if they have more power than they really do. They seldom fool anyone for long. And then there are the aggressive types who fight for dominance, getting into blatant public power struggles that only make them appear silly and immature.

One common mistake is to give domineering people more power than they should have, simply because they wear you down. Several years ago, I was helping some young managers in a nonprofit organization to plan their annual staff retreat. Every time I made a suggestion, they would look at one another and ask, "What would Colleen think about that?" Knowing that their bosses were named Paul, Ted, and Bob, I was a bit confused. "Who is Colleen?" I finally asked. "Oh, she's the receptionist," they replied. (I am not making this up.) These relatively new managers had apparently allowed themselves to be completely intimidated by an overly assertive employee.

Another power failure occurs when people shy away from valuable leverage-building opportunities. Krista, a rather unassuming client, recently sent me a rather unassuming e-mail. For several months, we had been working on a complex project that was now ready to be presented to her company's executive team. "I don't believe I should attend the executive session," Krista wrote, "because I haven't been able to go to all the project meetings." Excuse me? Did I just hear the sad sound of a leverage-building opportunity slipping away? Instead of worrying about appearing presumptuous, Krista should eagerly seize this chance to increase her exposure to the executive group. Fortunately, she finally decided to attend.

Perhaps more damaging is the opposite tendency: trying to use power that you don't actually possess. At best, this can cause you to appear a bit foolish; at worst, it can cost you your job. Sometimes people blunder into this error out of ignorance. One of my favorite stories along this line came from a former colleague, a labor attorney named Rick, who was doing some pro bono work for a nonprofit organization that we will call Community Health Care. The nurses at Community Health Care had voted to form their own little union, which was not affiliated with the AFL-CIO or any other labor organization. Management was not too pleased about this, since they did not want a union contract, but the company was legally required to bargain with this group. At the first bargaining session, the nurses arrived with a list of demands and handed them to Rick. "The company can't agree to these," said Rick. "Then we won't sign a contract," replied the union leader. "Okay," said Rick, and he got up and left. After several weeks, the puzzled nurses finally realized that they had no power to make demands—only to bargain toward a contract. And since "bargaining" means give-and-take, their refusal to sign a contract had actually stopped the negotiation process, making management very happy. They rather sheepishly called Rick to arrange another meeting. The moral of this story is that you should always be aware of the extent of your power. If you want to look ridiculous, just try to use power that you don't have.

Ego and arrogance also cause people to overestimate their power. A friend of mine once worked in a small consulting firm owned by two partners. Over the years, he and the three other staff consultants had developed close relationships with many clients, thereby making a significant contribution to the success of the business. When the consultants asked if they, too, could eventually be considered for partnership, the owners foolishly said no. Shortly thereafter, the consultants left to start their own company, taking their knowledge, experience, and client contacts with them. I'll let you guess which business is currently more successful.

Power mistakes sometimes spontaneously erupt from lapses in emotional control. During a tense meeting with the CEO and several other managers, Mary Ann, a young executive, was becoming angrier and angrier. Finally, after a particularly sarcastic remark from the CEO about her quarterly results, she loudly declared that she was not going to be treated that way, left the table, and slammed the door on her way out. Bad idea. When the other person's nameplate says CEO, you're going to lose the argument even if you're right. Fortunately, Mary Ann had built up some political capital, so the only immediate consequence for her was a referral to an executive coach. Someone with less leverage would undoubtedly have been fired.

WHAT IS YOUR POWER HISTORY?

Power mistakes are usually triggered by our temperament and our history. As anyone with multiple siblings or children knows, people are definitely not a blank slate at birth. Some of us are hard-wired to be more aggressive, while others are innately more reticent. Our reactions to power are also learned, however. And personal power lessons always begin at home.

Family dynamics are all about power. Perhaps you were taught that good little girls and boys quietly comply with whatever Mommy asks them to do. Or maybe you found a role model in Dad, who strictly enforced rules and harshly punished the slightest infraction. Perhaps you were the bossy oldest sibling or the defiant youngest. On the other hand, your parents may have helped you learn how to share power by involving you in decision making, and your sibling interactions may have taught you to cooperate and compromise. Experiences growing up vary widely from person to person, but, whatever your own childhood lessons about power, I can assure you that they are well entrenched in your personality. They are affecting your current behavior, for better or worse.

Behaviors acquired at home often resurface at work because the power relationships are so similar. As kids, most of us had a Mom, a Dad, and some combination of brothers and sisters. At the office, we now have a boss and an assortment of co-workers—and those who choose to become managers even acquire some "children." Many years ago, in the book, *I'm OK—You're OK*, Dr. Thomas A. Harris described three emotional positions from which we relate to others: Parent, Adult, or Child. At work, of course, we are expected to consistently operate as Adults. But despite being physical and chronological grown-ups, many people automatically lapse into their familiar Parent or Child behaviors. Ben, a corporate vice president, constantly shifted back and forth between Parent and Child mode. Whenever another VP strongly disagreed with him in a meeting, he would shout, curse, and pound the table—in short, Ben threw a tantrum. Afterward, he would meekly apologize to his boss, just like a naughty little boy. Small wonder that both his manager and his colleagues were getting a bit impatient with Ben. Yet his staff absolutely adored him because he protected them from upper management demands and always took their side in disagreements with other departments. Ben operated as a Child with his peers and boss, but was a Parent with his staff—and an Adult with absolutely no one.

Culture also plays a role in our reactions to power. Western cultures, such as the United States, tend to value individual achievement and to reward assertive behaviors, such as standing up for yourself, expressing opinions, suggesting improvements, and pointing out mistakes. Eastern cultures, on the other hand, emphasize group harmony; they value cooperative behaviors like listening, collaborating with others, striving for consensus, and showing respect for authority. When placed in the opposite culture, Westerners can resemble raging bulls, while Easterners may seem like timid rabbits. To succeed in a different culture, you must model the accepted power behaviors—an observation confirmed by many of my Asian clients who have come to work in the United States.

MEN, WOMEN, AND POWER

A recent column in our local paper described "gender tensions" following the election of our first female county commission chair, a petite woman who replaced a six foot seven man. After years of working with male, female, and mixed-gender groups, I have no doubt that a few tensions did indeed accompany this transition. For reasons of biology and socialization, men and women often have different approaches to power. The male power style focuses on dominance and hierarchy. In all-male groups, the members will quickly, although often subtly, establish a pecking order. No one may ever mention it, but everyone knows who's the top dog— and who's on the bottom. That's why physical size and strength often give men a few extra power points. The criteria for being the alpha male will shift with the situation, however. My husband manages a recreational baseball team, whose members come from a wide variety of occupations. But on the team, status derives almost solely from batting average—the mechanic who's hitting .350 definitely has more status than the physician batting .143.

Women, on the other hand, approach power differently, building relationships and looking for connections. Female groups may eventually develop some status differences, but that's not where they start. Put a group of unfamiliar women together and they will immediately try to discover what they have in common. Although overt expressions of dominance are frowned upon, women often exercise power through inclusion and exclusion. They are much more likely than men to play Shunning Games, for example. While the male power dynamic is "up or down," the female version is "in or out." Practical jokes and friendly put-downs provide an interesting example, because they are almost the exclusive property of men. Women hardly ever engage in either of these exchanges, since the aim of both is one-upmanship. Men, conversely, often know little about each other's personal lives, since they feel no need to connect in that way.

If you're thinking that these are broad generalizations, you are absolutely right. Because individual power styles are also shaped by family history, temperament, and culture, you do find women who use a "male" style, and vice versa. The most effective people borrow the best from both approaches, developing a more androgynous approach to power. The basic gender differences are still quite common, however, so anyone trying to operate with Political Intelligence should take them into consideration.

A frequent power problem in all-male groups is that the preoccupation with dominance often impedes collaboration. Each member may feel that others have no right to interfere in his "territory," so everyone limits conflict by operating autonomously. If you never collaborate, then you automatically avoid situations where you might have to give up some of your power. In all-female groups, problems are more likely to result from entanglement in relationship "issues": who's friendly or unfriendly, who's gossiping too much, who's getting more attention, who's being too critical, and so on. Interestingly, these matters are often put aside if someone has a personal crisis. Squabbling women can become quite supportive when health or family issues arise. (Men, of course, can also offer mutual support—but they may not know that anything is going on.)

Most groups, of course, are composed of men and women, and, most of the time, everyone gets along just fine. But because of the style differences, men sometimes view women as weak, while women occasionally see men as overbearing. Any group member who is the lone representative of a gender may have some adjusting to do. One of my clients was the only woman on an all-male management team whose members were constantly engaged in verbal pissing contests (an unquestionably male expression). To be a full participant in these discussions, she had to learn to speak up and stand her ground. The real challenge for a woman in any male group is that she has to walk a fine line. While she must adopt some characteristics of the male power style in order to be respected, she still needs to retain enough female traits to avoid being seen as a gender deviant. She has to be "one of the guys" without really acting like a guy. The higher a woman rises, the more important this balancing act may become, because most executive groups are still largely populated by men. On the other side of the equation, I know one gentleman who joined an all-female department after he retired from the military. As you might imagine, the gossiping and little snits among his colleagues nearly drove him nuts. "Why can't they just forget all that stuff and focus on work?" he exclaimed one day. Another male manager had a short tenure in a largely female health-care organization because he could never adopt a more relationship-oriented style. Women at all levels, including the CEO, found him to be "too aggressive."

When acting in accordance with their natural styles, men and women alike can inadvertently give power away. In the presence of someone they view as the alpha male, men may become overly submissive and deferential. I have a very clear snapshot in my memory of a group of highly paid, expensively dressed senior vice presidents gathered on a stage around their CEO, who was preparing for a presentation. They might as well have been panting, drooling, and wagging their tails. I honestly can't imagine a group of women executives surrounding a female CEO that way. But women have power problems of their own, which are frequently reflected in the way they talk. Women are often much too tentative and conditional in their speech: we should *probably* do this, we *might try* to take this approach, *maybe* we should reconsider. When they have definite opinions, women need to make definitive statements. Women also have a tendency to politely defer to men, allowing them to interrupt and take over the conversation. Finally, women sometimes overapologize. I occasionally work with a highly competent woman who says "I'm sorry" in response to almost anything, thereby automatically putting herself in a subservient power position. When I pointed this out one day, she seemed a little irritated by the feedback—but at least she didn't apologize!

So to summarize, your own personal power profile has developed from your innate temperament, your early role models, the culture in which you grew up, and some gender-specific behaviors. Because we each have our own automatic, built-in responses to power, you can greatly increase your Political Intelligence by learning to modify any knee-jerk reactions that might lead you into hazardous power mistakes.

MAPPING THE POWER GRID

Suppose you are the quarterback on a football team. To win, you need to not only sharpen your own skills, but also evaluate the ability of your teammates to support you and the ability of opposing players to flatten you like a tank. The political game works the same way: to achieve your goals, you need to know who can help you and who might hurt you. Instead of reviewing weekly game films, however, you are observing the playing field on a daily basis, trying to assess the relative power of those around you. And because power shifts frequently, you must be on the alert for trend lines. Collaborating with a fast-track superstar can reap valuable dividends, but be wary of anyone whose career appears to be in a tailspin.

To provide a method for organizing power assessments, let's create a Power Grid (shown opposite) that considers two factors: **Level of Position** and **Degree of Influence**. Level of Position is easy to rate, because it simply reflects the hierarchy: the CEO gets a 10, the lowest-paid employee a 1, and everyone else is distributed accordingly. Degree of Influence requires a more subjective assessment. You need to evaluate how many people someone knows, how highly the person's opinion is regarded, how many opportunities he or she has to interact with others, and so forth. To determine a particular person's power level, you must do the following: (1) Assign the person a rating on both Level of Position and Degree of Influence. (2) Add the ratings together to get a total Political Power Score. A successful CEO might get the highest score (twenty), while a poorly performing mail clerk might get the lowest (two). (3) Find the point where the two ratings intersect to place the person in a power category.

Power Grid

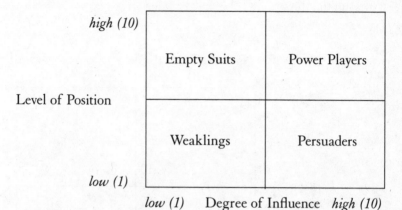

The categories on the grid represent four power combinations. Politically speaking, those on the left side of the chart don't have much firepower. **Weaklings** are low-level, low-wattage employees who may be perfectly competent, but have little influence outside their own job responsibilities. **Empty Suits** have high-level positions with impressive titles, but not much else. These are the jobs where politically ineffectual executives go to die. Although Empty Suits and Weaklings don't offer much as allies, you may still enjoy working with them. If they appear to be political suicides, however, keep your distance.

For a power boost, you need to cultivate the folks on the right-hand side of the chart. As allies, they can be most helpful—and you certainly don't want them as adversaries. **Persuaders** are what sociologists call "opinion leaders." Although they don't hold high-level positions, they can influence the views of many people. If you are in a lower-level job, Persuaders are probably your most useful allies because they are fairly accessible. It's easier to chat with the CEO's assistant than with the CEO. **Power Players**, of course, are the political superstars. Only a real Dimwit would ever intentionally antagonize a Power Player. And within the category of Power Players, you find the **Power Elite**, an exclusive little cadre of executives with extensive authority and widespread influence. They truly run the show.

Power Grid

high (10)	11	20 Power Elite
	10	
Level of Position		
low (1)	2	11

low (1)   Degree of Influence   *high (10)*

The more clearly you understand the goals and expectations of the Power Elite, the more likely you are to succeed. You should therefore pay close and ongoing attention to any Power Elite member who can affect your future. In a small business, this means everyone at the top. One of my client organizations is a family-owned furniture store with two owners, three managers, and fifteen employees. If they're smart, every single employee in that store will clearly understand the priorities of those two owners. In larger organizations, however, each job is linked only to specific Power Elite members. An accounts payable supervisor, for example, probably doesn't need to know much about the vice president of sales, but should definitely keep an eye on the CFO.

THE POWER ELITE CREATE THE CULTURE

An organization's culture is largely determined by the beliefs, values, and preferences of the Power Elite. This realization hit me when I experienced the dramatic change that accompanies the arrival of a new CEO. The transformation in the company was like having your mother's body taken over by a space alien: it still looked like your mother and sounded like your mother, but in reality your mother had become a very different, and possibly hostile, being. This massive culture shift was due solely to the dissimilar values and work styles of the two executives. The former CEO was gregarious and outgoing, had an engineering and marketing background, and was extremely close to his wife and three children. The new CEO was reserved and analytical, had a finance and consulting background, and lived alone. His first year produced marked changes in everything from business strategy to accounting practices to hours of work. There was a major turnover in the Power Elite as well: he fired all the top executives, thereby creating additional culture change in every department. Such a large-scale adjustment is stressful, tiring, and a royal pain. But for political success (and sometimes for survival), you must adjust to the culture established by the reigning Power Elite. There is not one chance in a million that you are going to change it.

Some people expend a great deal of time, effort, and energy fighting a hopeless battle against the culture. When Diana first became a project manager, she was determined to deliver projects on time and within budget. She soon discovered, however, that no one else paid much attention to either schedules or expenditures. Because of changes made by various executives, including the president, every single project experienced delays and cost overruns. To address this problem, Diana introduced a structured project management process with strict timelines and due dates. But nothing changed. With each overdue project, Diana became increasingly unhappy, irritable, and argumentative. The executives began to complain that she was uptight and obsessive. In her determination to make everyone do things the "right" way, Diana completely failed to recognize that her Power Elite group values flexibility and ingenuity more highly than they do structure and consistency. They would be much happier with a project schedule that builds in time for exploring new ideas and changing plans. Unless she can adapt to the prevailing culture, Diana's political stock will undoubtedly continue to decline.

When the culture seems uncomfortable or "wrong," give yourself a reasonable amount of time to adjust. Then, if you still feel like a misfit, you may need to move on. Putting a person into a company is kind of like an organ transplant. Sometimes the new part turns out to be compatible, and sometimes not. Just as the body will eventually reject an incompatible organ, a company will eventually "reject" an incompatible member. Some transplants just don't take. So if the values of the Power Elite seriously conflict with your own, you need to take your talents elsewhere. Otherwise, the stress will ultimately make you sick or drive you to some politically suicidal action.

Careful observation and a little detective work can help you determine the values of your own Power Elite members:

1. **Don't just listen to what they say. Watch what they do.** Why do the public pronouncements of all companies sound exactly the same? Because they all want to project a positive image. Don't rely on press releases or the annual report to clarify the true values of the Power Elite. Only an insane executive would ever publicly say, "Customer service is somewhat important, but we're really much more interested in getting their money," or "We don't want to do anything illegal, but we do want to use as many accounting tricks as we can." Actions are much more revealing than words. Do they care about customers? Watch the staffing level in the customer service department. Is quality important? Take a look at the acceptable error rate. Do they really mean that stuff about work/family balance? Check out how many managers are coming in on Saturday.

2. **Notice what they like to talk about and how they work.** People tend to talk about things that interest them. So if you have opportunities to chat with the Power Elite, take note of the topics that turn them on. A vice president who enjoys discussing new programs and innovative ideas is likely to appreciate creative suggestions, whereas one who gets excited about procedures and policies may welcome efforts to standardize operations. Personal work habits also provide a clue. Does your CEO work long hours? Always start meetings on time? Like to brainstorm new ideas? Spend time getting to know people? A personal work style often reflects what someone expects of others.

3. **See who gets recognized, praised, or promoted.** The Power Elite control various types of rewards, so notice where those rewards go. One of my clients was recently told by her vice president that she should look to a particular colleague as a role model. Even though she personally believes that this colleague is a moron, she needs to recognize that the VP views him differently. Her boss is trying to send her a message about what he thinks is important and is probably suggesting some changes in her behavior as well.

4. **Ask your boss or connected colleagues.** If you seldom have direct contact with the Power Elite, then learn from those who do. Cultural coaching is one of the most valuable contributions that a mentor can make to your career (so select a mentor who has enough sense to make accurate observations). If your boss is a decent human being and reasonably bright, he or she is your most obvious and available source of inside information. As long as they know you won't repeat their candid remarks, bosses generally love sharing their views. It's a kind of therapy for them.

5. **Observe what they change.** When someone new joins your Power Elite group, remain hyperalert for anything that signals a shift in the culture—or in what's expected

of you. I once worked in a department that experienced a major change in decision-making style with the arrival of a new vice president. Whereas his predecessor had liked face-to-face discussions and quick decisions, the new VP preferred written proposals and consensus-building processes. This was neither good nor bad, but it was definitely different—and we all had to adjust our behavior accordingly.

Sometimes, however, you get mixed messages. When two extremely powerful people have conflicting goals, priorities, or values, the result is a confusing and politically hazardous situation. Here's a common example: an experienced CEO decides to appoint a president to handle day-to-day business operations. Perhaps the CEO wants to spend more time on strategic issues or has decided to retire and wants to groom a successor. But a funny thing happens when the new president actually begins to make decisions: the CEO suddenly discovers that giving up power is difficult, marking the beginning of an uncomfortable and unproductive power struggle. Picture a couple of bull elephants fighting for dominance of the herd. If you see this happening, watch out!—you are entering the political danger zone. For a while, you and your colleagues, like the elephant herd, will have no idea which way to turn. The good news is that these conflicts are always time-limited, since no organization can operate with this kind of tension for long. The winner will be determined by the relative power of the combatants. But because underlings can't always accurately assess the leverage equation at the top, your wisest course is to lay low, offend no one, avoid taking sides, keep your opinions to yourself, and just wait it out. Believe me, you'll know when it's over, because someone will be gone.

Personal Politics

How Much Power Do You Have?

Assessing your situation:

- Think of someone you regard as a role model for exercising power and influence wisely. Now compare yourself to that person in the areas listed below. Use the following scale:

3 = Definitely   2=Somewhat   1=Not Really

Myself	Power Builders	My Role Model
3 2 1	Has responsiblity for results that are perceived as valuable	3 2 1
3 2 1	Is included in or consulted about important decisions	3 2 1
3 2 1	Is allowed to make independent decisions about their work	3 2 1
3 2 1	Has information or skills perceived as valuable by management	3 2 1
3 2 1	Has access to important or influential people	3 2 1
3 2 1	Has contact with people in many parts of the organization	3 2 1
3 2 1	Is trusted with confidential information	3 2 1

Myself	Power Builders	My Role Model
3 2 1	Is involved in important projects	3 2 1
3 2 1	Has expertise that is hard to replace	3 2 1
3 2 1	Is listened to by others when speaking	3 2 1
3 2 1	Appears confident and self-assured	3 2 1
3 2 1	Is well-regarded by people at all levels	3 2 1
3 2 1	Turns disagreements into productive discussions	3 2 1
3 2 1	Conveys interest and enthusiasm about work	3 2 1
3 2 1	Includes other people in decisions and activities	3 2 1

Moving from assessment to action:

- Look at the items on which you gave yourself a low rating. What could you do to increase your score in that area? If you scored your role model high on any of those items, what can you learn from that person's behavior? Might he or she agree to become a coach or mentor for you in that area?

- Think about the Power Elite in your organization. List the results, values, and behaviors that seem to be rewarded by this group. (Remember to consider what they *do*, not what they say.) Do you need to make changes in order to be perceived more positively by Power Elite members? If their values and priorities don't match your own, are you in the right organization?

What Is Your Power Profile?

Assessing your situation:

- Consider the factors below that may affect the way you react to power. Give some thought to your "power lessons" and how they influence your behavior at work.

Natural Temperament Do you tend to be more aggressive, calm, or anxious?	This is my nature:	So this is what I tend to do:
Family Members Consider mother, father, siblings, or other influential family members. How did they use power or react to power?	This is how power was dealt with at home:	So this is what I learned:
Current Relationships Consider spouse, significant others, friends, children. How do they use power or react to power?	This is what I experience in my current relationships:	So this is how I react:

Gender Behaviors How may you reflect the expectations that society has of male or female roles?	These are the gender expectations that I perceive:	So this is what I tend to do:
Culture How is power used in the culture in which you grew up? In the culture you are in now?	These are the cultural expectations that I have learned:	So this is how I react:

- What kind of "power mistakes" are you most likely to make? Are you too controlling and dominant or too reticent and afraid to use power? Do you defer too quickly? Or become too aggressive? What would you like to change about (a) the way that you handle power yourself or (b) the way that you react to others with power?

Moving from assessment to action:

- Identify the specific power situations that may cause you to make power mistakes. Do you get frustrated in meetings and react aggressively? Do you get easily intimidated by managers and give in too quickly? Do certain people just seem to activate your unhealthy power reactions? Determine how you will handle these situations differently in the future. Practice these behaviors until they feel comfortable.

Part III

HOW TO BECOME
A WINNER

Chapter 8

Increasing Your Political Power

When you think about your own political situation, you probably have something in mind that you would like to accomplish. Perhaps you hope to achieve certain career objectives or resolve some dilemma at work that is driving you crazy. Or maybe both. Whatever your current concerns, here's an important fact to keep in mind:

To achieve any goal, you must have sufficient power.

Having a sense of power is important, because people who feel powerless almost always feel hopeless and trapped as well. Hopeless, trapped people don't contribute much to the greater good; they typically spend a lot of time wishing things would change, but seldom set any specific goals. If you need help differentiating an unrealistic wish from a realistic goal, try a political power check. For instance, you might wish with all your heart that you could get rid of your boss, but you probably don't have the power to pull it off. However, you almost certainly have the power to make that relationship better if you choose to do so. Dumping your boss is a wish; improving communication with your boss would be a goal. Enhancing your political power will automatically increase the number and variety of goals that you are able to achieve. If you are a Winner, the desire to increase your power is not merely self-serving, since you will always be working for the success of the business.

THE FOUR P'S OF POLITICAL SUCCESS

Although "politics" is a pretty fuzzy term, there is a clear formula for political success—and it does not involve sucking up, groveling, or backstabbing. If everything is rolling along smoothly in your working life, that's terrific. But if not, the Four P's of politics can help you put together a Political Game Plan to improve the situation:

- **Power Assessment:** How can you improve your leverage position?
- **Performance:** How can your work make the business more successful?
- **Perception:** How can you enhance your reputation, especially with those who can help you achieve your goals?
- **Partnerships:** How can you increase your network of allies and supporters?

By thoroughly evaluating these four factors and making necessary improvements, you will automatically increase your political power. Does this formula guarantee a quick and painless solution to all your problems? No. Ruthless honesty and difficult changes are often required. But the reward is that you are more likely to achieve important goals and feel in control of your life. As we focus on increasing your power, however, you must remember the Political Golden Rule: *Never advance your own interests by harming the business or hurting other people.*

GAYLE'S POLITICAL PROBLEMS

To illustrate this Four P's formula, let's examine one person's political dilemma. Gayle is a technical publications supervisor in an electronics company, responsible for producing the instructional manuals packaged with all company products. When I first encountered her, Gayle was like a powder keg ready to explode at the slightest spark. She absolutely radiated stress, frustration, and anger—and a great deal of that anger was directed at her boss. Here are the wishes she expressed during our initial conversation:

- I wish things were done in a more planned and orderly fashion around here.
- I wish that my group was more involved in product planning.
- I wish product managers wouldn't dump work on my staff at the last minute.
- I wish I had a title that matched my responsibilities.
- I wish my boss would try to help me solve some of these problems.

If Gayle ruled the universe, she would immediately make radical changes in her job, her company, her colleagues, and her boss. As it is, she feels completely helpless to change anything. So, using the Four P's, let's diagnose her current political situation and see what she could do to increase her power.

- **Power Assessment:** To evaluate Gayle's leverage, we must consider both position power and personal power. Although she has little direct authority, Gayle's job in technical publications does afford some position power. While producing manuals is not a "glamour job," the fact that they are seen by every single customer is a potential leverage booster. Because all product-related information converges in the manual, Gayle has connections with many people throughout the company. Unfortunately, her chronic frustration and anger have diminished Gayle's personal power, because everyone tries to keep any interaction with her as brief as possible. Gayle could really use some support right now, but she has alienated most of her potential allies.

- **Performance:** Performance is definitely Gayle's greatest political strength, due to her department's reputation for consistently producing high-quality work under extreme time pressure. The company hardly ever receives complaints about the manuals created by Gayle and her staff. Although writing manuals may not be glamorous, the importance to customers is evident.

- **Perception:** On the positive side, Gayle is universally viewed as thorough, conscientious, and dedicated to customer service. Nevertheless, perception is a problem for her on two levels. First, the difficulty of her work is greatly underestimated. Few people really understand how much time and effort it takes to produce a complete, accurate, and comprehensible manual for the company's complex products; nor do they realize how much extra work is created by last-minute changes to a product's name or features. Second, and more important, Gayle is widely considered "difficult to deal with." When describing her, people use words like stubborn, intimidating, frustrating, harsh, impatient, and critical. She clearly does not have the reputation of a political Winner.

- **Partnerships:** Gayle is definitely not adept at forming partnerships. When discussing any problem, she quickly becomes adversarial and confrontational, in part because her frustration level is always so high. Because she lacks the authority to make the changes she desires, Gayle badly needs the cooperation of others. The "others," however, see no evidence that she is open to compromise on any issue.

In addition to lacking Political Intelligence, Gayle is probably something of a Martyr. She is currently so consumed by anger that she could easily be headed for political suicide. Gayle desperately needs a Political Game Plan.

The Performance Principle

True political power is based on valued contributions.

To become a political Winner, you must produce results that make the business more successful. Unfortunately, we have all seen some apparent exceptions to that rule: the highly connected, highly paid lamebrain who doesn't really do anything useful or the cute little cupcake who gets whatever she wants because she's very cuddly with her boss. Sometimes people do receive benefits that they haven't earned. One of my personal favorites was a rather nerdy guy with dandruff, who suddenly showed up one day as our company's new "governmental liaison." We had never had a governmental liaison, mainly because we didn't need one. This fellow, however, was not only given a six-figure salary, but the company also paid to ship his three horses across the country. He was a fairly harmless guy who spent his days doing . . . well, something. He walked around a lot. I think I forgot to mention that he was a cousin of the company president. These scenarios obviously provide more evidence that "life's not fair." As we have already established, however, fretting too much about fairness only wastes energy that could be put to better use.

But let's think about such situations politically for a moment. Because they add little value to the business, these parasites actually have limited leverage. Their political power and their ultimate fate are completely determined by their association with one particular person. The cupcake will only do well as long as her boss is successful—or until he finds another playmate. The above-mentioned cousin suddenly disappeared when the president retired (as did the need for a governmental liaison). Without value-added performance, these slackers have little control over their own future—and the resentment they engender in others is a definite political liability once their protector is gone. True political power develops from a track record of significant business contributions.

DEVELOP AN ROI MIND-SET

Implementing the Performance Principle requires an **ROI (return on investment) mind-set.** ROI simply means that every monetary investment is expected to return certain benefits and is therefore evaluated on how well those expectations are met. To your organization, you clearly represent an investment on two levels: management made the first investment decision when they created your position, then another when they hired someone with your particular experience and qualifications. Although they may never have been clearly stated, expectations do exist about the return that you should provide. Here are some questions to consider: Do you know why your organization decided to invest in you? Do you know what return management expects? Do you know how to maximize that return? To increase your political power, you must deliver more than the minimum expected ROI.

Applying ROI to your own position may seem a bit odd, because managers seldom think or talk about jobs this way. If you say to your boss, "What does this company expect from its investment in me? And how can I maximize that return?" she'll probably look at you a little oddly and wonder if you were paying attention during your last performance review. However, evaluating your personal ROI requires a broader view than simply understanding your current work objectives: you need to know how you, in your particular role, can make the company more successful. Let's take a couple of examples. Remember Greg, the tax specialist from the previous chapter who rose to become vice president? Greg could have met basic expectations for his first tax job by simply ensuring that the company complied with all applicable regulations. But, thinking with an ROI mind-set, what else can a tax specialist do to increase his company's success? For one thing, he can know federal, state, and local tax law so thoroughly that he is able to advise management on the tax implications of any decision. Because money saved on taxes goes straight to the bottom line, Greg's comprehensive grasp of the tax code visibly contributed to the company's financial success and increased Greg's political power as well. By becoming a regular participant in most high-level management decisions, Greg acquired broad business knowledge and greater visibility with the Power Elite. A clear convergence of personal and organizational goals, the sign of a true Winner.

Having a specialty may give Greg a slight advantage, but any job can be viewed with an ROI mind-set. Let's consider a more common, less specialized position: customer service representative (CSR). These are the folks who typically spend their days on the phone solving problems for unhappy, stressed, and frustrated customers. A manager bright enough to consider personal ROI might say this to a group of CSRs: "You are a crucial link between this company and our customers. To them, you are the face (or voice) of this business. You can influence their decision to purchase our products in the future. Collectively, you probably know more than anyone else about what is making our customers unhappy." Because few managers think like this, my guess is that most CSRs never hear that speech. They are more likely to be told to shorten their customer calls. Even if no one else sees the potential of this position, however, a CSR with an ROI mind-set will have a more enlightened view. With that ROI attitude, he will make every effort to give customers a positive impression of the company, solve problems quickly and accurately, and find opportunities to promote company products. If obtuse Power Elite members see customer service as a necessary evil that sucks up money, a few CSRs with an ROI mind-set might change that opinion, increasing their own political power in the process.

Developing an ROI mind-set means thinking like a business owner and seeing how your part fits into the whole. The more you learn about overall business goals and the activities of other functions, the more your perspective will expand. For example, customer service reps who understand the needs of the sales and accounting departments will be more likely to recognize and share useful information—like unusual complaints about a new product or a sudden increase in billing inaccuracies. These helpful actions will automatically gain them political points in the areas of Perception and Partnership as well.

Apart from your position, you should also consider the ROI expected from you, personally. Unless you're a relative of the CEO, you apparently have experience or abilities that someone felt would be especially useful in your job. Why did they choose you over the other fourteen people who may have applied? Have you ever asked? The answers may reveal some hidden expectations—and clarify the most important ones to meet. Of course, if you've been in your current slot for some time, this question may be less relevant. But if you're getting bored with your daily grind, perhaps a different question is in order: How could you get management to change their investment in you—that is, to use you in a different way? You may need to expand their view of your potential contributions.

DELIVER THE GOODS

Having an ROI mind-set can help you spot opportunities to increase your value, but you also have to deliver the goods. For starters, you need to understand what is particularly important to management, beginning with your boss. Whether or not you like your manager, respect your manager, or agree with your manager, remember this Organizational Fact: *Your boss has control over much of your life*. Understanding her goals and preferences is therefore a high priority. You must also recognize the values and priorities of the Power Elite. While your boss certainly has the greatest impact on your immediate circumstances, the people above her may control your future. Should you determine at any point that management's values differ greatly from your own, then you are in an uncomfortable situation. An experienced software engineer did not agree with some of the shortcuts in product design required by his VP of engineering. A young project manager found that the highly traditional company where he worked did not value his innovative ideas and creative approaches. When such differences begin to make work unrewarding, the best solution may be to find a more compatible environment.

With a change in management, the perception of your contributions may also shift. So following any turnover in leadership, you might need to recalibrate your priorities. During my years in human resources, I worked with three CEOs in the same company who all valued different aspects of the employee relations function. CEO #1 truly believed that employees were the heart of the business. "Take away the people," he used to say, "and all you have left are empty buildings and idle machines." When we proposed a quarterly employee breakfast, where he could interact directly with a group of "regular folks," he enthusiastically approved the idea. His successor, CEO #2, preferred written communication and greatly appreciated the letters, announcements, and newsletter articles crafted for him by our department. CEO #3 was more interested in information about employees than in the employees themselves, so he quickly became engrossed in the data from our employee-opinion survey.

Once you're doing the right things, then you must be sure to do them right. In any job, this means focusing on fundamentals. If you want people to feel that you add value, then you must produce quality work, meet deadlines, follow through with commitments, and anticipate and prevent problems. When anyone thinks of you, the words "reliable" and "dependable" should always come to mind. However, you can only deliver outstanding results if your innate abilities and talents are a good match for the requirements of your position. You will never excel in a job for which you are inherently unsuited. Neal, a salesman who had been failing spectacularly for nine years, provides a sad example of such a mismatch. The expected ROI for salespeople is pretty

clear: sell as much as possible and develop positive, lasting customer relationships. Successful salespeople are usually outgoing,
assertive, persuasive individuals who love to interact with people.
Neal, however, was just the opposite: a quiet, introspective, analytical fellow who enjoyed working alone and solving complex technical problems. From childhood, Neal had heard his father say
that sales was the path to success. So upon leaving college, with
this paternal directive burned into his cerebral cortex, Neal went
in search of a sales job and started down the road to failure and
depression. The first step in Neal's Political Game Plan was to
start preparing for a career change.

The Perception Principle

Invisible contributions have no political value.

Imagine this scene: a crowd is gathered in front of a burning
house. Suddenly, a teenage neighbor bursts through the front door
carrying two young children to safety. Cheers erupt, a television
reporter gets the young hero on camera for an interview, and the
story is carried on the evening news. The news report is seen by
the president of a local civic organization, which decides to give
the teen a college scholarship in recognition of his bravery. This
scholarship changes his life by allowing him to eventually complete medical school and become a skilled, respected surgeon.

Now rewind this heartwarming story to the beginning and
change one detail. While the crowd gathers in front of the burning house, the teenager carries the children out the *back* door and
puts them down on the lawn. The kids rush to the front yard to
find their parents, and the teenager follows a short distance behind. No one realizes that he actually rescued the children. No
TV report, no civic organization, no scholarship, no medical
school. This is a clear example of the Perception Principle in ac-

tion: outstanding performance only has political value if the right people know about it.

Some people are quite content to toil behind the scenes with little notice, and that's just fine. Others, however, feel unappreciated and neglected and believe that someone should be paying more attention to them. They say things like, "No one has any idea how hard I work" or "Nobody recognizes the challenges in this job." Anyone who engages in this kind of whining is striving mightily to become a Martyr. If you want people to know more about what you're doing, then you need to stop complaining and start looking for ways to increase their awareness.

Perception is important, because most of us have goals— either personal or organizational—that cannot be met unless people with power support them. Several years ago, I was asked to do a workshop for a group of county Clean & Beautiful directors. The mission of Clean & Beautiful organizations is to enhance the appearance of communities—by planting flowers on downtown streets, for example, or getting people to quit tossing trash out the car window. In one workshop activity, the directors were asked to think of someone with whom they had a politically difficult relationship and describe the world from that person's point of view. After giving this some thought, one director, whose county manager was his "politically difficult" person, exclaimed, "You know, I just realized that my program is not even on his radar screen!" If this Clean & Beautiful guy wants more program funding, then he needs to attract the attention of the person who controls the budget. All Winners recognize that the positive perception of an accomplishment is almost as important as the accomplishment itself.

MAKE YOUR VISIBLE RESULTS "SPARKLE"

When you go to a play, your opinion of the performance is shaped by the actors, costumes, scenery, props, and anything else within view. You never see the jumble of wires or pile of clothing lying behind the curtains. The same is true of your work. If you want a standing ovation, then the visible parts of your job need to "sparkle"—that is, catch people's attention in a positive way. In my own business, the spotlight usually shines on presentations, coaching sessions, survey reports, meetings, and promotional materials. If we want clients to think of us favorably—which, of course, we do—then the visible parts of our performance need to send the right message. Fortunately, our supply room is rarely seen by anyone.

"Visible results" refers to any part of your work that is viewed by other people. This may be a report, a design, a prototype, a presentation, an event—or some less tangible product like your participation in a meeting. One way to think about the "sparkle" factor is to categorize your work by level of visibility and importance, giving you the four groupings below.

	high Importance *low*	
high	*Starmakers* Be sure that results "sparkle."	*Maintenance* Standardize with a reliable, quality template.
low	*Transparent Tasks* Look for ways to increase visibility.	*Time Wasters* Give these activities a low priority.

Visibility

High-importance, high-visibility activities are **Starmakers**, with significant potential for increasing political power. Starmaker activities exist in every job. If you are asked to plan a company luncheon, make an executive presentation, or solve a tough technical problem, put some effort into making your work memorable. Serve a special dessert after lunch, create an attractive format for the executive handouts, present your solution to the technical problem at a staff meeting. But you must be careful. The objective here is not to become an annoying braggart or obnoxious show-off, but to do quality work in a way that creates positive perceptions. If that difficult technical problem isn't relevant to your colleagues' work, then don't share it at the staff meeting. If it is, though, you have an ideal opportunity to be helpful and "sparkle" at the same time.

On the other hand, activities that are highly visible, but low in importance, represent **Maintenance**. Simply be sure that they are carried out reliably enough to avoid attracting negative attention. I think of this as the "clean bathroom phenomenon"—no one will notice if you keep your bathroom clean, but everyone will notice if it's dirty. Low-importance activities fade into the background unless something gets screwed up. Those routine reports that you submit every month aren't remembered by anyone—except for that one time that the wrong data went to the CEO. Creating standard processes, procedures, or templates is usually the best approach to Maintenance work, leaving you more time to "sparkle" at less mundane activities. Any task low in both importance and visibility is a **Time Waster** that should either be eliminated or receive only the minimum attention necessary. These chores have no political payoff.

Sometimes, for one reason or another, important work is relatively invisible. With these **Transparent Tasks,** your goal is to get them into the spotlight. If a task truly is significant, you can find legitimate opportunities to increase its prominence. One frequently useful strategy is to mine these invisible assignments for interesting information. Facts, figures, and data act like bait for managers, who tend to be information junkies. If you want them to pay attention to anything, give it a number. Developing measures for your Transparent Tasks will almost always increase their (and your) visibility. In human resources, for example, we routinely dealt with employee complaints, which could range from a simple gripe about a supervisor to a formal charge of discrimination or sexual harassment. Management never paid much attention to this important aspect of our work unless the situation deteriorated and lawyers became involved. But once we started counting and classifying these employee issues, then using that data to create a quarterly report, management suddenly began to take notice. Eventually, I presented this information to executive staff meetings throughout the company. Once you have increased the visibility of a Transparent Task, then you can start to work on the "sparkle" factor.

Finally, you need to double- and triple-check all visible work for accuracy, quality, and appearance. If you are a manager, please recognize that you are judged by the performance of everyone in your domain. I know one CEO whose executive assistant, a bright and efficient young woman, has the unfortunate habit of sending out e-mails without proofing them first. The inevitable misspellings and grammatical errors not only reflect badly on her, but also on her boss—and, in fact, on the whole company. Errors, omissions, or general sloppiness will cause people to make negative assumptions about your performance in other areas. Imagine for a moment that you are getting on a plane. As you board, you notice that the paint is peeling, the fabric on your seat is ripped, and the lock on the overhead bin doesn't latch. Are you starting to get just a tad uncomfortable about the engines? A small printing business near my office provides an excellent bad example. A large sign on the building lists their services, including "Commerical Printing." I don't think we'll be taking any print jobs there in the foreseeable future.

ACT LIKE THE PERSON
YOU WANT THEM TO SEE

Your thoughts and feelings are known only to you. Other people base their perceptions on your behavior, because that's all they see. Whether you feel confident and comfortable doesn't really matter, as long as you can act that way. When people are learning new roles or trying to change their behavior, psychologists often recommend a technique called "acting as if"—so if you're not accustomed to public speaking, try acting as if you were; if you don't like your boss, try acting as if you do; if you've never made a sales call, try acting like a confident salesperson. After a while, it may no longer be an act.

People in unfamiliar roles often suffer from the imposter syndrome, feeling that they don't really belong in their new position. This is true of new managers, new salespeople, new trainers, new anything. But the secret is to keep acting the part until it feels comfortable. To pull this off, you must have a clear mental picture of the person you want to portray, so you need to find a role model. Whenever coaching clients are trying to make a behavior change, I recommend that they find someone who provides a good example and study them, identifying exactly what they do that seems to work. Many years ago, I used this technique in my first management job. Although I had been to a zillion staff meetings, the idea of leading one made me nervous—so I just decided to "play the part" of my former boss. Before long, running staff meetings became routine. Sometimes you can even be your own role model. If you want to develop a better relationship with a difficult colleague, for example, observe how you act with people you like—then "act as if" you like this more challenging person.

Acting like the person you want others to see can also help you achieve your career goals. If your objective is a promotion or a career change, then you should try to talk, dress, and act like someone who would fit the new position. If you want to become a vice president, wearing your Birkenstocks and brown-bagging your lunch will probably not help—unless, of course, that's what VPs in your company do. In which case, you shouldn't be caught dead in a three-piece suit. Consciously shaping your image does not mean that you are being shallow and artificial. You are simply trying to remove any barriers that might keep people from seeing your qualifications.

Trying to be something you are not seldom works. Striving to appear confident and qualified often does. If you make a speech and attempt to fake your knowledge of the topic, people will see right through you and you will appear foolish. But if you know your stuff, acting like a confident and comfortable speaker, despite the butterflies in your stomach, will create a much better impression. Because people make decisions based on what they observe, successfully managing perceptions is a sure sign of Political Intelligence.

The Partnership Principle

Every positive working relationship
increases your political power.

You can increase your political power geometrically by developing a **Partnership** approach to your work. For some, Partnering comes naturally; others have to work at it. Beth was a natural relationship builder whose job in advertising brought her into contact with many people. Having noticed that she was never around at lunchtime, I once asked Beth where she usually ate. "Oh, various places," she replied. "In fact, I try to meet a different person for lunch every day. I get to know people so much better that way." If eating lunch with five different people each week is your idea of hell, don't worry. Less gregarious people simply need to identify their most important contacts. Regardless of how many working relationships you have, you should tend them all carefully. Every time you snap at someone, react defensively, or fail to cooperate, you are giving away a little bit of your political power.

INVITE PEOPLE TO YOUR PARTY

Few, if any, jobs can be performed in isolation these days. A blacksmith shoeing horses in the Old West might accomplish a full day's work on his own, but now such autonomous jobs are virtually nonexistent. We all depend on other people, and other people depend on us. Unfortunately, however, the instinct to protect and defend turf is quite strong. This natural tendency creates problems at work, because territoriality usually provokes others to respond in kind. When people fail to collaborate, the business automatically suffers. To implement the Partnership Principle, you need to put aside your territorial impulses and think in terms of involvement and inclusion. If you're working on a project, who else might contribute? If you're making a decision, who might have useful information? If you're making changes, who needs to know about them? If you have information, who else might find it helpful?

When you develop the habit of inviting people to your party, you increase your political power and usually improve the quality of your results. The director of clinical services in a psychiatric hospital asked her staff physicians to try prescribing a new type of medication. After several weeks, however, only a couple of prescriptions had been written for the new drug—not too surprising, because physicians aren't exactly famous for taking orders. Once she realized that her unilateral decision hadn't produced the desired outcome, the director decided to appoint a medication review committee composed of both doctors and nurses, giving them the power to recommend medication changes. By creating this group, she not only developed a more effective mechanism for reviewing drugs, but also increased her allies among the medical staff. Organizations are simply networks of people, so every association links you to another source of knowledge, expertise, or assistance. Your own immediate and future goals will determine which contacts are most helpful. When you have those contacts, use them! During a recent coaching session, a client mentioned that he hoped to transfer to a different division in his company, so I asked if he knew anyone over there. After he named a few people, I said, "Have you talked with them about your interest in moving?" He stared at me for a few seconds and replied, "Actually, no. I can't believe I never thought to do that."

Sometimes we simply forget to reach out to people, but in other situations we create unconscious barriers. Higher-level managers, for example, may often be more accessible and interested than people assume. An early mentor taught me this lesson when I was a district manager in a government organization. I mentioned offhandedly one day that it would be nice if my staff could meet the head of our agency, an intelligent, thoughtful gentleman named Claude Myer. "Then why don't you invite him to a staff meeting?" asked my mentor, thereby turning my vague wish into a specific goal. I did, and he came. In fact, he thoroughly enjoyed meeting everyone and said he hoped to visit the field offices more often. Remembering this incident, I can recall the momentary shock I experienced upon realizing that it had never even remotely occurred to me to call up Mr. Myer and invite him to the office. That experience taught me an important lesson about the unthinking limitations we sometimes place on our own power.

The Partnership Principle may also lead you to "joint ventures" with other departments or organizations. Joint ventures are particularly useful when two functions have complementary knowledge or skills. Engineers who design products can gain valuable information from salespeople about customer habits and preferences. Training departments that want to "sell" their programs and services internally can learn some useful lessons from the marketing folks. Such collaborations produce twofold political rewards, simultaneously improving your results and increasing your network. Partnering is especially smart when you share common goals with another group. Harold, the new executive director of an organization that helps people who have disabilities, discovered that relationships between his agency and others with a similar mission had grown increasingly antagonistic and competitive. These supposedly charitable organizations were implementing redundant programs, competing for limited funds, and trashing one another in the press. To Harold, it seemed painfully obvious that all this territorial bickering did nothing to help the disabled population. In the year that followed, he met frequently with the other agency heads, encouraging them to work together for increased program funding, legislative changes, and favorable publicity. These efforts resulted in improved services to their client group—and as an additional benefit, Harold greatly enhanced his professional reputation and acquired a supportive network of allies. People with common goals automatically increase their political power when they band together.

STRETCH YOUR TOLERANCE ZONE

Even if you are a kind, amiable, inclusive person, I'm willing to bet there are certain people you simply do not want to invite to your party, no matter what. Whenever you try to work with them, you wind up frustrated, aggravated, or disappointed. Because we all tend to feel that our own way is the right way, we often have limited tolerance for people who do or see things differently. However, the fundamental lesson of the Partnership Principle is this: the more people you can work with, the more your power will increase. A wide tolerance zone gives you a definite political advantage.

Unless you are dealing with a complete Dimwit who can't get along with anybody, your frustration with a co-worker may well be the result of work style incompatibilities. Because people are born with different brain chemistry, raised with different values, and exposed to different life experiences, it's not surprising that we have different ways of approaching tasks and projects. But certain pairings seem to inevitably lead to predictable problems. The table below lists some of the most common work style opposites. See if any of your own difficult relationships reflect one or more of these differences.

Work Style Opposites

Producers	Empathizers
Producers want to get right to work and focus on results. Their enjoyment comes from the tasks they do. Relationships are seen as a distraction from the work.	Empathizers like to get to know their colleagues. Their enjoyment comes from working with others. Relationships are seen as an integral part of the work.
Empathizers see them as insensitive and boring.	*Producers see them as touchy-feely and overly sensitive.*

Visionaries	Implementers
Visionaries are motivated by the possibility of creating a better future. They are interested in formulating long-range plans and exploring new possibilities.	Implementers are motivated by the desire for current work to be done properly. They want to be sure that details are taken care of and immediate problems are solved.
Implementers see them as out of touch and impractical.	*Visionaries see them as short-sighted and unable to think strategically.*

Planners	Movers
Planners want to develop well-thought-out plans for solving a problem or implementing a project. They like to assess costs and benefits,	Movers want to take immediate action when confronted with a problem or a project. They like to quickly implement solutions, learn

Planners	*Movers*
anticipate roadblocks, and develop contingency plans before taking action.	from the results, and make corrections as needed.
Movers see them as slow and overly cautious.	*Planners see them as rushed and impulsive.*

Controllers	*Independents*
Controllers want to be sure that everything happens as expected and that people do what they are supposed to. They like to direct the actions of others.	Independents like to work on their own without interference. They want to understand the goal to be achieved, then be left alone to accomplish it.
Independents see them as autocratic and power-hungry.	*Controllers see them as resistant and uncommunicative.*

Organizers	*Adapters*
Organizers are good at bringing order out of chaos and creating policies, procedures, and systems. They feel most comfortable working in situations where the structure and expectations are clear.	Adapters are good at adjusting to change and quickly shifting direction when necessary. They prefer working in an environment that is not highly structured and allows flexibility.
Adapters see them as obsessive and uptight.	*Organizers see them as disorganized and careless.*

Innovators	*Traditionalists*
Innovators enjoy coming up with new ideas and finding ways to improve products and processes. They find change stimulating and interesting. They like working in situations where creativity is encouraged.	Traditionalists value time-tested methods and approaches. They like to find a process or solution that works and stick with it. They value stability, predictability, and consistency.
Traditionalists see them as flighty and unrealistic.	*Innovators see them as unimaginative and dull.*

Stretching your tolerance zone to accommodate work style opposites will pay dividends beyond better working relationships. Ironically, the people who annoy us the most tend to be our natural complements. They have strengths that we lack, and vice versa. Collaboration with your opposite will often produce a better product and provide a role model for some new and useful skills. The trick is that you must continue to remind yourself that this frustrating colleague is not wrong or incompetent, just different from you.

GAYLE'S POLITICAL GAME PLAN

Gayle, the stressed-out technical publications supervisor, was eventually able to put aside her anger and craft a Political Game Plan, becoming a true political success story. When I saw her six months after our first meeting, she seemed like a different person: relaxed, smiling, and happy. After mentioning that she had recently been promoted to director, she reported that her relationship with her boss had greatly improved. "I don't know that he's changed much," she said, "but maybe I'm acting differently with him. I used to just complain all the time about things that were really out of our control. Now I've finally accepted that planning and orderly procedures are just not part of this company's culture and probably never will be."

Gayle pulled off this miraculous transformation by making a conscious and concerted effort to increase her political power. First, she stopped passively wishing for change and started working on the following list of goals:

- Stop complaining so much about management and the company.
- Become more involved in the product-planning process.
- Work with product managers to create a more orderly system for changes.
- Understand and meet the requirements for being promoted to director.
- Develop a better working relationship with my boss.

As part of her Political Game Plan, here are some things that Gayle did:

- Accepted the unalterable reality that she was a structured, orderly person in a chaotic, disorganized company. Instead of continuing to rail against the culture, she started looking for situations where her planning and organizing abilities could make a contribution.
- Initiated a dialogue with the product managers. She first helped them understand the problems created by last-minute changes to the manuals, then involved them in creating a more systematic process for making these adjustments.
- Asked if she could attend product-planning meetings. Hearing product plans from the beginning gave her a better understanding of what would eventually need to be included in the manuals.
- Recognized that her anger and irritation had seriously reduced her leverage with important allies. She began to

listen more attentively, consider different points of view, and generally make her communication with others less confrontational.

- Changed her behavior with her boss. Instead of blaming him for all her problems, she took a more "partnering" approach and asked for his help in modifying some of their work processes. She also tried to better understand the challenges that he was facing.

- Asked the HR department about requirements for being upgraded to a director position. Upon discovering that she was already functioning at that level, she prepared a justification for a title change, which her boss agreed to support.

- Perhaps Gayle's most interesting decision related to some of her associates. "I used to have lunch every day with a 'support group' of other women managers," she said, "but I suddenly realized that they spent all their time complaining about management. And they were particularly negative about my boss. We never tried to help each other solve problems or develop strategies. It wasn't a support group at all—it was just a bitching club! So I started eating lunch with other people. If I had kept listening to that bunch, I never would have made director."

Gayle began her political rehabilitation when she stopped complaining and engaged in some rigorous self-examination. Then she developed a realistic game plan to increase her political power. The energy that had previously been tied up in all that unproductive anger could now be focused on accomplishing her goals. By giving herself a political makeover, Gayle succeeded in transforming herself from a Martyr to a Winner.

Personal Politics

How Can You Use the "Four P's"?

Assessing your situation:

- Start by defining your current goals, since your energy should be directed toward achieving them.
- Answer any of the questions below that might be helpful in increasing your political power and accomplishing your goals.

POWER ASSESSMENT

Leverage Boosters	**Leverage Busters**
What factors are increasing your leverage? How can you capitalize on them?	What factors are reducing your leverage? How can you overcome them?

PERFORMANCE

Develop an ROI Mind-set	**Deliver the Goods**
What can you do to improve management's perception of your ROI?	What can you do to deliver expected results more reliably or dependably?

PERCEPTION

Make Results "Sparkle"	**Acting "As If"**
Which of your activities need to become more visible? More creatively presented or delivered?	How can you change your behavior to match the way you want to be perceived? Or the role you would like to have?

PARTNERSHIPS	
Invite People to Your Party When could you appropriately increase others' involvement in your decisions, projects, or activities?	**Stretch Your Tolerance Zone** With what type of people do you find it most difficult to work? How can you work more effectively with them?

Moving from assessment to action:

- Turn the answers to the above questions into an action plan. List specifically what you plan to do and when. Set a time to follow up and assess your progress.

Chapter 9

Sharpening Your Influence Skills

Most people, most of the time, operate on autopilot. They proceed through the day doing whatever comes naturally. Sometimes things go their way and sometimes not. In a sense, they're unconscious—of their own behavior, of their effect on others, of any point of view except their own. Unconsciousness is not a problem when you're ordering a hamburger at McDonald's or picking up your clothes at the cleaners. Such routine, low-impact transactions don't require or deserve any real investment of energy, thought, or planning. Few interactions at work fall into this category, however. Successfully getting through the day in a complex corporate environment requires a fair amount of conscious attention.

To compare conscious and unconscious behavior, let's consider that McDonald's order. Under normal circumstances, you probably follow an automatic, mindless pattern for this mundane transaction—walk in, place your order, hand over the money, get the food. You do it the same way every time, usually while thinking about something else. But suppose that today the McDonald's counter clerk turns out to be your CEO's teenage daughter. Suddenly you're thinking about everything you say and do: "Good to see you again! How are you doing? How is school? [Oh no! My T-shirt has a sex joke on the back!]" And as you walk backward toward the condiment stand, if you discover that she gave you the wrong burger, you'll probably plan exactly what to say when you take it back. The McDonald's order has now become a conscious transaction.

You began monitoring your ordering behavior because the stakes in this situation have been raised. Rather than hungrily waiting to get your burger and go, suddenly you're considering how your words and actions might affect your career. Even if she never gets your order right, I doubt that you'll be rude to this particular clerk. And you may never wear that sex-joke T-shirt to McDonald's again. In a small way, you want to influence this girl: you want her to think well of you. To influence anyone, you have to give some thought to what you're doing. True political geniuses consistently make conscious, intelligent decisions about their behavior. It's tough to become a Winner if you're walking around in a coma.

THE IMPORTANCE OF SELF-MANAGEMENT

To earn your black belt in influence skills, you must be a master of self-management, because this is the only way to make wise decisions about your behavior. When you wish to influence another person, you're usually hoping that *they* will change. But instead, you should first consider how *you* might change, because you can only control your own actions. My extremely wise mother taught me this lesson when I came home from college for a holiday visit. After several days of listening to complaints about how my roommate was driving me crazy, Mom looked me in the eye and calmly said, "You know, you probably can't change her. All you can change is your attitude toward her." To my surprise, this advice actually made all the difference. When I became more friendly and accepting, my roommate began to act differently as well, and we eventually became fast friends. Here's the Paradox of Influence:

To get other people to change their behavior,
you have to change your own.

Interpersonal interaction is like a dance. If you and your partner are doing the tango, your steps will automatically fall into an established pattern. To shift from a tango to a waltz, one of you has to break the pattern and get into a new rhythm. Similarly, we have habitual patterns in our interactions with other people. If you want someone to act differently at work (or at home, for that matter), you must first change your own "steps." Let's take a simple example: Brad, who is extremely outgoing and talkative, goes to lunch with Frank, a quiet and reserved colleague. Predictably, the following pattern develops: Brad does all the talking, while Frank sits and listens. Later that day Brad complains to a friend: "Frank hardly said a word at lunch today. I wish he'd speak up every once in a while. What a boring guy!" Frank, on the other hand, describes the encounter somewhat differently: "Brad never stopped talking at lunch today. I wish he'd shut up occasionally and let someone else get a word in. What a boring guy!" Because Frank was quiet, Brad kept talking to fill up the silence. Because Brad was talking, Frank waited patiently for his turn to speak, which never came. Had either one changed their behavior, a different pattern might have emerged. Frank would probably participate in the discussion if Brad ceased his monologue and asked a few questions. Brad might listen if Frank would only speak up. To shift the pattern, at least one of them has to engage in a little self-management.

Mastering self-management means developing three skills: (1) self-observation; (2) self-control; and (3) selective behavior. **Self-observation** means that you are always aware of what you're doing. Although this doesn't exactly constitute an out-of-body experience, you do need to scrutinize your actions with the eye of an outside observer. During his one-sided conversation with Frank, a self-observant Brad might be thinking, "I'm certainly talking a lot. Could that be why Frank is so quiet? The more I talk, the less interested he seems. Maybe I should stop talking and ask him a question. What could I ask him about?" **Self-control** is a concept that everyone understands, but many fail to practice. Simply put, self-control means the ability to put on the brakes, to rein in your impulses. You consciously decide not to do something that you want to do or say something that you want to say. While walking through the company cafeteria after lunch one day, Eileen stopped to talk to a colleague about an issue involving their new boss. "Boy, Jack's a real little dictator, isn't he?" Eileen exclaimed, unfortunately conveying that sentiment to everyone within earshot. For talkative souls, developing self-control often means putting a filter between their brain and their mouth. At the other end of the spectrum, Carlton, the new president of an electronics company, would become so deeply lost in thought that he walked right by people without even seeing them. Employees quickly spread the word that Carlton was arrogant and unfriendly. For him, self-control meant maintaining some contact with reality when he was around other people. The final component of self-management is **selective behavior.** If you can observe your actions and restrain yourself from doing what comes naturally, then you are in a position to increase your influence by making better behavioral choices. Carlton, for example, might want to try saying "good morning" when passing someone in the hall. Eileen, instead of publicly proclaiming her unhappiness, might choose to occasionally mention some of her new boss's good points. Successfully mastering self-management will put you in control of your behavior and prevent you from inadvertently drifting into the Dimwit category.

THE PROCESS OF INFLUENCE

For any ability you can name—playing basketball, painting portraits, making speeches, performing mathematical calculations—there are three categories of people: those who are blessed with natural talent, those who can become competent with training, and those who will simply never get it. Although a few do seem to have a natural genius for influence, most of us fall into the "trainable" group. Influence training begins with an understanding of how the process operates.

The Influence Process

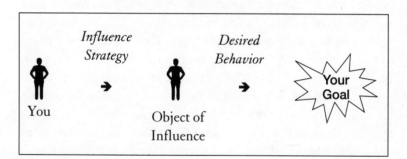

- You have a goal that is important to you.
- Another person can help or hinder your accomplishment of that goal.
- To reach the goal, you need for that other person to engage in certain behaviors.
- To produce these desired behaviors, you must use the appropriate influence strategy.
- If you choose the wrong strategy, the person may not want to help you.

If you are worried about becoming overly manipulative, remember that the Political Golden Rule prohibits you from using any influence strategy that could be harmful to the other person. Assuming that your goals are worthwhile, encouraging others to help you accomplish them is simply smart. Actually, acting *without* thinking usually does more harm to others, which is why we refer to rude and offensive people as "thoughtless."

Let's use a few simple examples to illustrate how this influence process works:

- Darren would like to have the experience of working internationally. His boss is currently overseeing an important project in Germany that requires someone with his particular skills. Although Darren has dropped several hints, so far his boss hasn't asked him to participate. What might he do to motivate his boss to send him overseas?

- Vivian's garage is a mess, primarily because her husband's stuff is strewn all over the place. Vivian would like to have a clean garage and feels that her husband should be the one to clean it. He doesn't seem to be making any moves in that direction, though. How could Vivian influence her hubby to start tidying up the clutter?

- Jake's girlfriend has announced that the two of them should probably see other people "for a while." Jake would prefer to continue their previously exclusive relationship, but she seems fairly adamant about her position. What behavior on his part might encourage his girlfriend to reconsider her decision?

All three of these folks have goals that involve another person who is not being immediately responsive. To make progress, they first need to recognize the difference between "influence" and "control." You can influence many, many things, but you control very little. Darren can't order his boss to send him to Germany, Vivian can't make her husband turn off the TV and head for the garage, and Jake can't force his girlfriend to stay away from other men. Attempting to exert control in these situations will only make things worse, whereas the right influence strategy might elicit willing cooperation. A CEO once told me that his greatest frustration was his inability to control what happened in his company. That may sound odd, but it's true. Although a CEO has tremendous power, he can't directly control all the decisions made by managers or the work produced by frontline employees. If he tries, he's just going to screw things up. Like everyone else, CEOs succeed by concentrating on the factors that they can influence— like the strategic direction of the company or the quality of executive management.

People often fail to achieve important goals because they waste valuable energy on things that are clearly out of their control. Gayle, the technical publications supervisor whom we met in the previous chapter, wanted to get rid of her manager and completely change the company culture. She obviously had no power to make that happen. Nevertheless, for quite some time Gayle diverted considerable energy toward complaining, arguing, and resisting her boss. Only after she shifted her focus to goals that she could actually influence, did she begin to get what she wanted. Because everyone has a limited energy supply, you need to aim for objectives that you have some realistic chance of accomplishing.

CHOOSING YOUR INFLUENCE STRATEGY

Once you shift your thinking from control to influence and from changing others to changing yourself, you can begin to make politically intelligent decisions about your actions and interactions with others. To become more influential, you must remember this:

You always have choices about your behavior.

Whenever you act without thinking, you give up your power to choose and often move farther away from your goal. If Vivian starts yelling at her husband about being such a slob, she's likely to wind up with an angry spouse, a ruined Saturday, and status quo in the garage. Yelling may allow her to release some pent-up anger, but it's probably not a helpful strategy for moving toward the clean-garage goal. How could she get him to start cleaning? Several possible strategies come to mind: (1) calmly and politely ask him to do it; (2) explain why the clutter bothers her; (3) suggest doing the cleaning together; (4) mention that she's planning to pay someone to clean out the garage; (5) explain that because she needs more space, she will be putting some stuff from the garage in the trash; or (6) offer to do some other unpleasant chore in return for his help with the garage. The point is, there are many options. Vivian needs to choose the behavior that is most likely to influence her particular spouse.

Politically intelligent people always seek a strategy that is both aimed at their goal and suited to the person whose help they need. What approach, for example, might convince Darren's boss that he is the right person to go to Germany? To answer that question, he should consider the boss's personality, goals, and decision-making style, as well as the needs of both the project and the business. When Jake's beloved drops the unexpected bombshell that she wants to see other people, how should he respond? His first impulse may be to beg, plead, and whimper that he just can't imagine life without her. But that would be self-defeating: his goal is to make himself more desirable, not less. Although it may accurately reflect his current emotional state, pathetic clinging behavior is pretty unappealing. A better initial reaction might be to keep his cool and say, "Okay, let's talk about that."

When one strategy isn't working, you need to shift your approach and try something different. Unfortunately, refusal and rejection often cause us to simply escalate our current behavior. We speak louder, plead more pitifully, or become more insistent in making our points. This is like shouting at someone who doesn't speak your language—raising the volume will not help them understand. If the other person seems to be tuning out your brilliant logical arguments, shift your focus and ask a question. Or if your subtle hints are being ignored, try directly stating what you need. The more tools that you have in your influence toolbox, the more successful you will be. One way to broaden your repertoire of influence behaviors is to watch what others do. During a visit from my newly married daughter, I had a problem with some household chore and called out for my six foot four husband. "John, I could really use somebody tall and strong to help with this," I said. My daughter looked at me with wide eyes and exclaimed, "So *that's* how you get them to do things!" Although I had given no particular thought to what I was saying, my choice of words apparently provided her with a new strategy to try at home.

UNDERSTANDING THE OTHER SIDE

To choose the best influence approach, you must consider the world from the other person's point of view. Each of us travels through life in our own little "box." That is to say, our view of the world is limited, or "walled in," by our values, beliefs, experiences, and goals.

Your View

As we peer out at the world through the walls of our box, everything we see is shaped by our own point of view. But to influence others, you have to mentally visit their box and see how the world looks to them. If you can develop the ability to adopt another person's viewpoint, you will have taken one huge giant step toward becoming a political Winner.

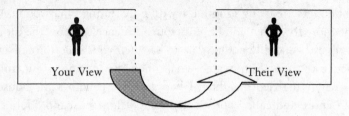

Let's consider the earlier example of Darren, who wants his boss to send him to Germany. From Darren's point of view, this trip would be an exciting journey, an opportunity to add international experience to his résumé, and possibly the next step toward a promotion. Speaking strictly from his own box, Darren might say to his boss, "I understand that you need to send someone to Germany to work on the Anderson project. I just want you to know that I would love to get that assignment. I've never been to Europe, so it would be awfully exciting for me. And I could really use the international experience. This would be a big step forward in my career."

But to understand his boss's view, Darren probably needs to consider these questions:

- What are his manager's goals for this project?
- What qualifications does she feel are important for this assignment?
- What is her opinion of his previous work?
- Might she have any reservations about sending him to Germany?
- Is there anyone whom she might consider more qualified?
- Who would handle his current responsibilities while he's gone?
- How would *her* boss view Darren's participation?

Pondering these issues might inspire Darren to change his approach: "I understand that you need to send someone to Germany to work on the Anderson project. I've been reviewing the project documents, and I think that my experience on our last two projects could really help to make this one work. We overcame some of the same obstacles that they seem to be facing, and I've already worked with several members of this project team. I know that you may have been considering Kevin for this assignment because of his international experience, but I have some ideas about how we might split the project duties to use both our talents. I could bring Wanda up to speed on my current projects so that she could fill in while I'm gone. What do you think?"

Exactly why is this strategy more likely to succeed?

- First, Darren has framed his request in terms of **shared goals.** Instead of being all about Darren ("It would be awfully exciting for *me.... I* could really use the international experience."), he stresses the success of the project, a much more pertinent goal for his boss.
- Second, Darren has made the effort to **anticipate objections and concerns.** He has recognized that completion of his current work could be an issue and identified Kevin as his strongest competition for the assignment.
- Third, he has tried to **assess the leverage equation.** Because his boss appears to have all the power in this situation, Darren hopes to boost his own leverage a bit by mentioning his previous experience with similar projects and his relationship with the project team members.
- Finally, he ends by **soliciting her point of view.** The best way to get inside someone else's box is to ask questions and really listen to the answers.

Although there's no ironclad guarantee that Darren's manager will agree, this strategy should definitely improve his chances of getting the assignment.

Suppose you find yourself in a situation where you feel absolutely certain that another person's idea, plan, or behavior is absolutely wrong. What then? This is when it is most difficult to see the other side—and when it's also most important to make the effort. In most conflicts, people are not disagreeing about the facts.

"They're wrong" usually translates as "they don't agree with my opinion." Keep this in mind:

Facts can be wrong. Opinions are simply different.

Apart from legal and ethical issues, the conclusion that someone is "wrong" is probably both inaccurate and politically detrimental. A county mental health agency acquired a new director who had a medical background. One of her first actions was to replace the agency's training program with a new curriculum based on a medical model. To the mental health managers—all of whom had been with the agency for at least ten years—this change was clearly wrong. They conveyed their negative opinions to the new director at every opportunity, complaining about the content of the training, the length of the program, and the fact that medical approaches had no relevance for mental health professionals. In response to their objections, the director immediately scrapped the new training program, right? Of course not. The managers' constant criticism did indeed convince the director that there was a big problem—but with the management team, not the training. If these managers really wanted to influence their new boss, they needed to consider her view of the situation and open their minds to some new approaches. Hammering people with your own opinion seldom changes anything. When you really try to understand other people's points of view, they will frequently reciprocate by listening to yours.

KEEPING YOUR EYES ON THE PRIZE

The ability to maintain a laserlike focus on your true goal is another critical influence skill. In complex and emotionally charged interactions, people often lose sight of their objectives and lapse into counterproductive behavior. Before becoming hopelessly entangled in these confusing scenarios, you must clearly define exactly what is most significant to you and keep your eyes on that prize. Whenever you become angry or frustrated, just continue to ask yourself, "What specifically is most important to me in this situation? What do I want?" and then manage your behavior accordingly.

I recently found myself in one of these tricky circumstances. A very intelligent but totally disorganized university professor asked me to help create a leadership development program for a large corporate client. My areas of program responsibility involved leadership assessment and teambuilding, with additional consultants handling a variety of other topics. As project leader, the professor was responsible for defining objectives, creating a program outline, managing the budget, and developing a schedule. Unfortunately, we all soon discovered that her organizational skills were nonexistent—but she saw no problem whatsoever. So what's the solution? Make her see the difficulties that she is creating? Try to take over the administrative tasks? The best course of action depends on my goal—and in this situation, my primary goal is simply to make a good impression on the client with my part of the program. I have no control over the rest of the curriculum or the management of the project. If I offended the professor, I might be taken off the project altogether, so I needed to (1) let go of my opinions about how a leadership development program "should" operate; (2) put up with the frustrations; (3) be a pleasant and cooperative colleague; and (4) do the best work I can within my areas of responsibility.

When people feel they are being criticized, they often employ diversionary tactics to distract you from your goal. Such distractions can take many forms, including anger, tears, excuses, or shifting the focus elsewhere. In the recreational baseball league that he manages, my husband, John, recently had to deal with a player who had threatened an umpire with physical harm. As soon as John brought up the matter, the player replied angrily, "That guy can't tell a ball from a strike! He gets calls wrong all the time. He shouldn't be an umpire at all! You need to fire him."

"That's not the issue here," said John. "The issue is that we can't have people making physical threats under any circumstances."

"But he cursed at me," the player shot back. "He shouldn't be swearing and taking the Lord's name in vain. I don't have to put up with that!"

"If that's the case, I'll talk with him about it," John said. "But the issue here is your own behavior. You cannot make threats to anyone. If you do, you can't play in this league." After a few more diversionary attempts, the player grudgingly agreed.

Sometimes, especially when emotions are running high, people get so carried away that they fail to recognize when their goal has actually been reached. While working on an important project, Marissa began to feel that the project manager was intentionally leaving her out of major decisions. Although she tried to discuss this with him on several occasions, he paid little attention to her concerns. By the time she finally complained to her boss, Carlos, Marissa had progressed from annoyance to full-blown fury. After agreeing to mediate the situation, Carlos met with the project manager to hear his version of events, then brought the two of them together to discuss the issue.

"Carlos tells me you're having a problem," said the project manager.

"I'm having a problem with you!" exclaimed Marissa angrily. "You completely ignore my suggestions and never invite me to meetings where the decisions are made. This project is getting really screwed up, and you don't seem to realize it!"

"So what is it you want me to do, exactly?" responded the project manager.

"I want to be involved in meetings about how the project will be implemented. My department will be the one using this new system, so we need to have input on how it operates," replied Marissa.

"That seems reasonable enough," the project manager said. "I have no problem including you in those meetings."

"But you have totally ignored all my suggestions about this project!" Marissa repeated. "Whenever I've tried to talk to you about it, you give absolutely no consideration to my point of view. I think that you're just . . ."

"Marissa," Carlos interrupted quietly, "I believe you got what you wanted, didn't you?"

"Oh," said Marissa, taking a deep breath. "I guess I did."

If you are not clear about your objectives—both long-term and short-term—then you will be driven by your immediate needs, wants, desires, and feelings. You may ultimately find that the greatest obstacle to achieving your goals is staring back at you in the mirror. To make a wise decision about your influence strategy, you have to know what you want.

BALANCING YOUR INFLUENCE TOOLBOX

A project team in an advertising agency is developing a new ad campaign for a client. Two members of the group, Paul and Donna, feel that the team needs to take a different approach to the project. At the next meeting, Paul brings up the subject. "I think we're making some mistakes here," he says. "Before we go any further, we really need to consider the objectives of this campaign. I'd like to describe a different strategy that I think may be more appealing to this particular client." After Paul finishes his presentation, Donna speaks up. "I sense some concern about Paul's comments and would like to hear what the rest of you think. Let's go around the table and get everyone's opinion." After listening carefully to all the responses, Donna summarizes what she heard. "It sounds as though people see some merit in Paul's ideas, but are worried about whether we can meet the project schedule if we change direction now. Is that correct?"

Donna and Paul exemplify two opposite influence strategies. Paul is using **direct influence**. He tells people exactly what he thinks and attempts to convince them that he is right. Donna, on the other hand, is using **indirect influence**. She watches people's reactions, asks questions, and learns from their responses. In your influence toolbox, direct and indirect skills are like a hammer and screwdriver: both are useful, but you need to use the right tool at the right time. If you only possess one of these implements, certain situations may be challenging. Driving a nail with a screwdriver can be tough.

Because most of us have a natural inclination to be either more direct or indirect, acting unconsciously automatically produces a heavier reliance on one set of skills and a failure to recognize situations that call for the other. Mistakes can be made in either direction. Ralph, the new director of a large department, attended many meetings during his first two months on the job. In all of them, he listened quietly, occasionally asked a question, never stated an opinion. Most of the time he sat away from the table or in the back of the room. People soon began to question his leadership ability. Vickie, on the other hand, was in a job where she had no direct authority over anyone, yet had to ensure that projects were completed on schedule. She dictated timelines to project participants, sent frequent e-mails telling them what to do, and argued about how their tasks should be prioritized. After a while, they just ignored her. Both Ralph and Vickie were simply overusing their natural style.

To optimize your influencing ability, you need to possess a full set of tools. That way, you will have a greater variety of choices available in any situation. A range of influence strategies is shown on the continuum below. First, decide which are most comfortable for you and which are most difficult, then determine when you might benefit from using the ones that you avoid or neglect. Once you start experimenting with these less familiar skills, be patient with yourself and don't give up. Developing any new ability takes time and practice. I doubt that you were able to drive a car the first time you got behind the wheel.

INDIRECT SKILLS			DIRECT SKILLS
Observe & Wait ➔	Ask & Listen ➔	Persuade & Convince ➔	Order & Act

Observe and Wait: The power of watchful waiting is often over-looked. My own role model for this particular skill was a col-league named Carl, who had mastered the art of The Perfect Moment. Several hours into a daylong committee meeting, led by a woman who had completely lost control of the group, most of the participants (myself included) were heatedly debating, argu-ing, and disagreeing. Carl, however, had hardly said a word. Fi-nally, just when we were about ready to start throwing coffee mugs at each other, Carl spoke up. "What do you think about this idea?" he asked, then proceeded to outline a plan that seamlessly combined our various points of view. By watching and waiting, Carl had been able to spot The Perfect Moment to introduce his suggestions. Because he had previously been so quiet, as soon as he spoke everyone else fell silent and listened with rapt attention. Sometimes, as they say, less is more.

To be a political Winner, you must learn to quickly process a constant stream of observations. Watching the daily ebb and flow of the political tides will help you detect conflicts, alliances, and lever-age shifts. During individual encounters, nonverbal signals can alert you to the feelings and reactions of the other party. In a meeting, monitoring the topic changes and interpersonal undercurrents may reveal The Perfect Moment to make your point. Accurate and timely observations are essential to the influence process, since they enable you to select the most effective strategy for each situation.

Waiting—the decision to postpone action—can feel like tor-ture to those who are naturally inclined to do something, any-thing, that feels like forward motion. But sometimes doing nothing is the wisest course. Art, a successful salesman, had un-fortunately acquired a boss who was a complete Dimwit. For sev-eral months, Art put his best sales skills to work on this manager, attempting to change her leadership style and improve their com-munication. He was in her office almost every day, working on their relationship. Sadly, all this activity only convinced her that Art was a pest. Art's talent for direct influencing had served him well in sales, but watchful waiting would have been a much better strategy in this situation.

Any strength carried to an extreme becomes a weakness. Too much waiting and observing will only convince others that you have nothing to say. If you are most comfortable when you can sit quietly and absorb the conversation, then you probably overuse this skill and need to practice being more direct. Does this mean that you should start yapping your head off in every meeting? Heavens, no. But you do need to recognize those situations where speaking up could help you achieve your goals. Once you spot such an opportunity, you must force yourself to overcome whatever fear is holding you back. If you're afraid that you might say something stupid, don't worry about it. You're probably screening your words so carefully that nothing remotely foolish could slip past your lips.

Ask and Listen: The very best consultants, counselors, and salespeople are all masters of asking and listening. They understand that the more you know about another person, the more influential and helpful you can be. Think for a moment about your own conversations. When someone else is speaking, do you actually listen or are you mentally rehearsing your reply? Really listening means being fully focused on the other person—not fidgeting, multi-tasking, or impatiently waiting for your turn to talk. You already know how to do this. Suppose your CEO walks in and says, "I have something very important to tell you." I guarantee that you will listen, with rapt attention. No need to waste your time or money attending a listening workshop—simply turn on your listening skills during any important conversation, not just those with the CEO.

Those who neglect their indirect skills often miss opportunities to fully understand others' concerns, problems, values, or opinions. But the true motormouths never even get to hear what other people might have to say. Their compulsive talking is so extreme that it appears to be a pathological disorder. They almost literally never shut up. If you are in this category, no one is likely to tell you—well, how could they?—but if this sounds at all like you, get some help. You will rarely influence anyone unless you improve your verbal self-management, because the more you talk, the less people hear.

The artful use of questions can be a wonderfully effective method for influencing others. To be meaningful, a question must be an actual inquiry, not merely a statement ending with a question mark. "I think this vacation policy is really stupid, don't you?" is not a real question. Nor is, "What idiot came up with the new vacation policy?" But, "What do you think of the new vacation policy?" actually asks for an opinion. In your influence toolbox, questions are like a Swiss army knife: they can be used in many different situations.

- **Exploratory questions** help you understand the other person's point of view and convey that you are interested in their experiences, opinions, or ideas.
  Example: A product manager wants to learn about customer reactions and decides to talk with a salesperson. Instead of saying, "I'll bet your customers love the new product line, don't they?" he should ask, "What have your customers had to say about the new product line?"
- **Involvement questions** aim to increase buy-in by inviting others to participate in a project or help plan a change.
  Example: A human resources specialist wants to implement a new dress code for employees. Instead of announcing, "We will be sending out a dress code to improve appearance in the office," she should first ask employees, "How would you define professional and unprofessional dress at work?" Then implement some of their suggestions.
- **Softening questions** reduce defensiveness and help you bring up a topic or get a point across in a less confrontational manner.
  Example: A project team member feels that the group is having too many meetings and has decided to bring this up to the team leader. Instead of saying, "You're wasting too much time having all these meetings," she should ask, "What would you think about reducing the number of meetings we're having?" Asking questions is a point-

less exercise, of course, unless you plan to listen to the answer.

Asking and listening can also be overdone. Too many questions, one right after another, can make the other party feel like a suspect under interrogation. And if you only listen, without ever sharing your own opinions, people may eventually decide that you have something to hide. The most effective communication is always two-way.

Persuade and Convince: How do con men (or women) separate people from their money? How do preachers inspire people to live right and do good works? How do recruiters get young folks to join the army and be all that they can be? By being persuasive, convincing, and masters of direct influence. If you give yourself high marks on indirect skills, then you may need to get more comfortable with the direct approach. To help you become more directly persuasive, here are ten tips to consider:

1. *Do your homework.* You will adopt the persuader role more comfortably if you are fully informed about your subject and able to answer questions intelligently.
2. *Speak up.* Psychic persuasion is seldom successful. Talking is usually required.
3. *Demonstrate confidence.* Should the car salesman start his pitch by saying, "I don't know if you're really going to like this model very much" or "This is really a great car"? You get the idea. Remember that confidence is conveyed not only by your words, but also by your tone, posture, and expression.
4. *Don't try to fake it.* If you don't know something, say so. Attempts at bluffing are usually obvious and just make you appear foolish and insecure. Truly confident people readily say "I don't know," then follow it up with "but I'll find out."

5. *Believe in your product*. Regardless of whether your "product" is an idea, a suggestion, a policy, or a program, you can only convince others of its worth if you are a believer yourself.

6. *Know your audience*. Exactly who are your objects of influence? Consider their background, experiences, hot buttons, needs, fears, and attention span. Then shape your communication accordingly.

7. *Look for shared goals and common interests*. Determine how your proposal would benefit the other party. "What's in it for me?" is the first question on anyone's mind. That's just human nature.

8. *Generate excitement!* Paint a mental picture. Tell a story. Catch their attention. Be upbeat and positive! After graduating from college, my daughter, an advertising major, began her letter to prospective employers with this opening line: "I'm quick, sharp, and smart! Hire me now while I'm still inexpensive." She got a lot of interviews.

9. *Get them involved*. If you drone on too long, people will tune you out and start thinking about what they want for lunch. Engaging them in discussion will hold their interest and make you more persuasive. You can't convince someone who has stopped paying attention.

10. *Don't forget your indirect skills*. The most effective persuaders also know when to shut up and listen.

Finally, always be on the lookout for role models. When you spot a master of persuasion, study any useful techniques and adapt them to your own style.

Order and Act: Sometimes you only get results by being extremely direct. During a recent workshop, the participants and I noticed an odd smell wafting into the room and found a work crew painting the patio outside our windows. I nicely explained that because the fumes were quite strong, we would appreciate their completing the painting after we left for the day. But when they came back half an hour later, with the smell worse than ever, a more direct approach seemed to be in order. "I need for you to stop painting now," I said to the crew leader. "If this is a problem, I will be glad to explain it to your supervisor, but we can't have any more painting while we're in this room." I stood there until they stopped. Being direct does not mean being rude or offensive, but it does mean being firm.

"Order and act" is an appropriate strategy whenever the situation calls for strong leadership. After being appointed to head a state government agency, Joan discovered that important fiscal policies were not being followed and that some managers were engaged in questionable ethical practices. She quickly issued new policy directives, installed tighter financial controls, fired the ethical offenders, and met with every management team in the agency to make her expectations clear. In these circumstances, an indirect approach would have been useless. Direct skills can also be helpful when a group lacks clear direction, has difficulty making decisions, or includes many inexperienced members. On the home front, use direct influence to set clear limits for children, let your spouse know what's bothering you, or assertively deal with annoying relatives.

Relying too heavily on direct skills can provoke resistance and defensiveness, because people may feel they are being inappropriately ordered around. If the term "control freak" has ever been applied to you, then you undoubtedly need to beef up your indirect influencing ability. Ironically, those who most want to take control are often the least influential members in a group, because others fear that they may be too power-hungry.

So what does it take to be influential? (1) An awareness of what you're doing and how others are reacting to you; (2) a clear focus on your goals in every situation; (3) the willingness to understand another person's point of view; (4) the ability to make conscious choices about your behavior and not be blindly driven by your emotions; and (5) a full set of influence skills to keep you from overdoing your natural tendencies.

Personal Politics

How Good Are You at Self-Management?

Assessing your situation:

- Using the chart below, rate yourself on your self-management ability.

	Almost always	Often	Seldom	Almost never
I am able to view my actions with the eye of an outside observer.	4	3	2	1
I am often surprised by the way others view my behavior.	1	2	3	4
I tend to act without thinking.	1	2	3	4
I am good at anticipating how people will react in different situations.	4	3	2	1
I am able to keep myself from saying things that might be unwise.	4	3	2	1

	Almost always	Often	Seldom	Almost never
I believe in "doing what comes naturally" so that I can really be myself.	1	2	3	4
I stop myself from doing things that could have negative consequences.	4	3	2	1
I often regret the actions that I have taken.	1	2	3	4
I say things to others without considering how they may react.	1	2	3	4
I find it hard to stop myself from doing things that I really want to do.	1	2	3	4
I am consciously aware of my actions and reactions around others.	4	3	2	1
I have tried to develop behaviors that are outside my "comfort zone."	4	3	2	1

	Almost always	**Often**	**Seldom**	**Almost never**
I tend to do things that are against my better judgment.	1	2	3	4
I make conscious choices about what I say and do with others.	4	3	2	1

Count the number of 4, 3, 2, and 1 scores that you gave yourself and put those numbers in the table below.

Higher Self-Management Skills		**Lower Self-Management Skills**	
Total 4's	Total 3's	Total 2's	Total 1's

The more scores you have on the left side of the chart, the better your self-management skills. (This assumes, of course, that you are able to evaluate yourself accurately, which is not always the case.) The more scores on the right side, the more problems you may encounter in this area.

Moving from assessment to action:

- Identify the times when your actions, reactions, or statements have created problems for you. Can you find any patterns in these situations? If you could relive them, what would you do differently? When do you feel you need to be particularly aware of your effect on others? List some specific behaviors that you might need to change.

Which Influence Skills Do You Need to Improve?

Assessing your situation:

- Think about the direct and indirect influence skills discussed in this chapter. For each category below, use a percentage to indicate how frequently you use each set of skills in influence situations. Your percentages should add up to 100.

Indirect Skills			Direct skills
Observe & Wait	Ask & Listen	Persuade & Convince	Order & Act

Moving from assessment to action:

- Do you tend to overuse either direct or indirect skills? In which categories do you need to improve? Set some specific goals for using new influence skills. In what situations or with which people do you need to use these skills? Decide what you will do differently the next time you are in these situations.
- Think of someone you would like to influence.

  (1) What is your goal in this situation? What do you need this person to do?

(2) Try to describe the world from the point of view of your influence target. What are this person's goals and problems? How would the person describe you? How would the two of you describe the issues about which you disagree? How do these viewpoints differ?

(3) Consider how you or others have tried to influence this person in the past. Should you try any new strategies? What strategies have not worked well? What approaches seem to work best with this person?

Chapter 10

Managing Power Relationships

In every organization, some people have more power than others. (You may recall this as an Organizational Fact of Life.) To get a snapshot of the formal power hierarchy, just look at the organization chart. You will clearly see three basic power relationships: above, below, and equal. These simple differences create some challenging problems, because many otherwise well-adjusted people have difficulty with certain power positions. Some can't stand being in the "below" role and automatically rebel against anyone in authority. Others work well with management, but have a tough time getting along with their peers. Those who feel uncomfortable in the "above" position often turn into buddy-buddy bosses who try to be best pals with their employees. Becoming a Winner means successfully managing relationships in all directions. If only that were as easy as it sounds.

THE "FULL CIRCLE" OF INFLUENCE

Imagine that a group of people are going to rate your work effectiveness. This group will include your boss, your colleagues, and (if you are a manager) your employees. You will also rate yourself. Then suppose you are given a report that compares all these responses—letting you see, for example, whether your boss and your co-workers view you the same way. How do you think it would turn out? This process is known as 360° Feedback, which many organizations use to help people get a clearer picture of the way they are perceived at work.

After looking at hundreds of these reports over the years, I can quickly tell when someone has a power position issue. Certain people get high ratings from everybody except their boss. Others receive low ratings only from their peers. Some managers get high marks from everyone except their employees. In each case, the person involved has trouble with one type of power relationship, but otherwise appears to be doing a fine job. Think about yourself. If you received a 360° Feedback Report, would people in all power positions view you positively?

- Would your boss describe you as helpful, cooperative, and easy to work with?
- Would your colleagues say that you regularly listen to other points of view, share information, and provide assistance willingly?
- If you are a manager, would your employees describe you as supportive, respectful, and willing to listen? Would they say you set a good example as a leader?

If you have any doubts about the answers, then you may want to examine your power relationships.

Power difficulties often grow out of the Parent, Adult, and Child roles that were discussed in chapter 7. Because power relationships at work often mirror those in families, certain events or circumstances can activate an entrenched Parent or Child reaction that overrides our normal Adult behavior. When this happens, our self-management skills vanish, we act unconsciously, and our ability to influence others is automatically diminished. Put more simply, we do some really stupid things.

Upward influence is a challenge for people who automatically view anyone in management as a Parent, then react like a Child, becoming either rebellious and hard to manage or submissive and overly compliant. Rebellious employees tend to be oppositional and antiauthoritarian, just like two-year-olds and teenagers. Chris, a social worker, didn't like policies, procedures, or rules. He argued about policy decisions and looked for any possible loophole to get around restrictions. If he didn't agree with a request made by his manager, Chris simply ignored it. He took the opposite position on almost any issue about which his boss expressed an opinion. Needless to say, his manager began to feel that a conversation with Chris was about as pleasant as a root canal, so he avoided him whenever possible. Chris had virtually no upward influence in his agency.

Submissive employees, on the other hand, are eager to please and afraid to disagree. Carson, a newly promoted engineering manager, was soft-spoken and agreeable. Before taking any action, he was always careful to check with his boss, and he never questioned his manager's suggestions, even if he had reservations. Although Carson's primary goal was to please his manager, the effect was quite the opposite. On a 360° Feedback Report, his manager wrote, "Carson needs to stop asking 'What *should* we do?' and start saying 'This is what we *ought* to do.'" Because he was reluctant to volunteer any opinion that did not feel completely "safe," Carson greatly reduced his upward influence.

Lateral influence problems arise when people take an inappropriate Child role with their colleagues, often reflecting childhood patterns with siblings and playmates: the competitive youngster who always has to win, the self-sufficient child who prefers solitary activities, and the playground bully who likes to push other people around. For competitive co-workers, life is a contest and winning is the goal. They have little interest in the needs, concerns, or problems of colleagues. Unless there is a clear and immediate personal payoff, teamwork and collaboration are viewed as useless distractions. During a department teambuilding session, Mark mentioned that Tonya, one of his co-workers, seldom returned phone calls or responded to requests for information. "I don't have enough hours in the day as it is," replied Tonya, "so why would I take time to do those things, when they have absolutely no effect on my goals?" A few months later, when Tonya desperately needed Mark's participation in a project, he was unavailable. Surprise, surprise. Some competitors are simply not helpful, but others are annoyingly self-promoting. These folks are usually easy to spot, because they consistently try to demonstrate superior knowledge and often attempt to horn in on others' projects, especially those that will increase their own visibility.

Solitary colleagues prefer to work on their own. Like lone wolves, they hate hunting in packs. Because they don't find interaction particularly rewarding, their enjoyment at work comes from the tasks, not the people. In their view, teamwork and collaboration interfere with more meaningful pursuits. Daniel was one of five training specialists in a government agency. When selecting workshops to teach, he looked for out-of-town sessions that involved a single instructor, so that he could travel by himself. Whenever possible, he used these trips to avoid staff meetings, which he felt were a complete waste of time. He spent many hours researching new material at a nearby university library, where he buried himself in the stacks with a pile of journals. Unfortunately, when budget cuts forced a staff reduction, Daniel's lack of involvement in departmental activities made him the most expendable person in the group. He was laid off. There is absolutely nothing wrong with enjoying independent activities, but too much solitude can be politically hazardous.

Bullying co-workers want to get their own way. If they can push others around a little, that only makes it more fun. Simon, a product design engineer, always argued forcefully for his position in design meetings, refusing to consider other alternatives or opinions. His views often prevailed simply because he wore everyone out with his vigorous attacks. Colleagues who noticed potential design problems seldom brought them to Simon's attention, knowing that even mild criticism would be met with a verbal barrage. Over time, Simon's reputation began to decline, as most product design failures could be traced to his ideas. Had he taken a more collaborative approach, both the products and his reputation would have been better served.

Downward influence is essential for leaders and managers. Because management tasks need to be performed by Adults, problems inevitably occur when managers operate in either Parent or Child mode. Parental managers come in two varieties: dominating and smothering. Dominating bosses overuse their direct authority by issuing orders, directives, and reprimands. Although they may comply, employees seldom respect these little tyrants. Daryl was one such manager. Whenever an employee displeased him, he would yell, "I might just have to fire you!" Finally, the entire staff confronted him as a group, pointing out that these threats weren't very helpful to morale. To which Daryl replied, "I may just fire all of you for this!" Although Daryl was obviously clueless, he wasn't really a bad guy—simply an insecure new manager who didn't understand how to use authority effectively. He eventually developed more self-confidence and became a better leader.

Smothering managers, who get intensely involved in the details of their employees' work, usually see themselves as concerned, conscientious, and helpful. But employees are more likely to view this hovering attentiveness as interference and micromanagement. Roberta, the manager of a district sales office, had smothering tendencies. She carefully reviewed her salespeople's reports, proposals, and travel schedules; asked them to copy her on all correspondence; and often accompanied them on sales calls. Not surprisingly, salespeople usually transferred out of Roberta's district as soon as a position became available elsewhere.

Managers who operate from the Child position are uncomfortable having authority over others. Because they worry about being liked, they try to be everyone's pal. Although most employees don't want a domineering boss, they don't want a spineless jellyfish either, so buddy-buddy bosses get little respect. Nell, a supervisor who received a 360° Feedback Report, was dismayed by low ratings from her staff. "I thought they liked me," she lamented, "but apparently they don't like me at all!" Actually, "liking" had nothing to do with it. Nell's survey results clearly showed that her employees wanted stronger direction, more feedback, and the resolution of some performance problems—in other words, they wanted Nell to act like a manager! Ironically, these were the very actions that she had avoided, fearing that they would make her less likable. Nell was learning a fundamental lesson of downward influence—that being respected is much more important than being liked.

If you see yourself in any of the above descriptions—or if you just want to further hone your influence skills—then check out the strategies below. As you've probably figured out, consistently operating as an Adult is a basic requirement for managing power relationships.

UPWARD INFLUENCE: MANAGING YOUR BOSS

Let's be honest—if you got to pick your boss, you might make a different choice. But in the real world you have to work for anyone who happens to be favored by management. Even a boss who is totally incompetent still has enough position power to make your life fairly miserable. So the more effectively you can influence upward, the more pleasant your days are likely to be. Toward that end, here are some suggestions for managing bosses in a politically intelligent manner.

1. **Accept the fact that your boss has been given the power to direct your activities.** This is true even if you are much

smarter than he is, even if you should have been given his job, even if he is the most obnoxious loudmouth on the planet. You are stuck with this boss for the immediate future, so becoming rebellious will only make a bad situation worse. Accepting reality and working to increase your influence will produce better results.

2. **Don't expect perfection.** Managers are people, not androids, so they have an endless variety of quirks and eccentricities and odd little habits. Recognize your boss's hot buttons and, for heaven's sake, don't push them! There's a name for people who annoy their managers on purpose—masochists. If you have a wonderful boss who is a pleasure to work with, celebrate! Be grateful every day for as long as it lasts. If not, lower your expectations.

3. **Study your boss's management style and figure out what makes her happy.** Look for clues that tell you how she likes work done or how she prefers to get information. If you're not sure what your boss expects from you, in terms of results, work habits, communication style, or anything else, then don't try to guess—ask! You need to find out ASAP. Any reasonable manager will gladly answer these questions and, in fact, will be pleased and surprised by your interest.

4. **Try to make your boss look good.** Produce quality results, meet deadlines, stay within your budget, respond to people quickly. Find problems that need solving and address them. Contribute new ideas and suggestions. Share useful information with your boss. Your own political power will grow when your manager tells everybody how wonderful you are!

5. **Never, never, never complain to others about your boss**—especially to people outside your department or to your employees (if you are a manager). Strategizing with trusted peers about how to handle your manager's more challenging peculiarities is one thing—kind of like a

group therapy session—but trumpeting your unhappiness far and wide will only get you in trouble.

6. **Give your boss a sincere compliment from time to time.** Managers hear lots of complaints, but few employees ever bother to give their boss a kind word. Unless your manager resembles Attila the Hun or Adolf Hitler, you can surely find some quality worth praising. Mention it at some appropriate point. But let's be clear—paying a sincere compliment is not the same as groveling or sucking up.

7. **Finally, don't forget the old saying, "It's not your boss who protects your job, it's your boss's boss."** Look for opportunities to interact with higher-level managers. If they know who you are and think well of you, then you will have enhanced both your political power and your job security.

Conflicts between employees and managers can be especially dangerous after a management change. Some people get used to one type of boss, have trouble adjusting to a different style, and angrily head down the road to political suicide. When the powers-that-be give you a new manager, recognize that the world has changed, so you'd better change with it. Unless you have enormous leverage, you will not be overthrowing your boss. Any hostility or resistance will only get you tagged as "hard to manage." One executive who inherited a rather antagonistic staff summed this up quite neatly: "Either people change or we change people." If you had the ideal boss before, that was good luck for you—but that's the past. Now you must figure out how to work with a different person, even if you're not happy about it. If you can keep an open mind, you may actually find that they have some new things to teach you. Some of my most valuable lessons were learned working for a nightmare CEO. I wouldn't particularly want to repeat the experience, but it was undeniably educational.

THE VIEW FROM THE TOP:
HOW TO WORK WITH EXECUTIVES

Managing your boss is one thing; working with executives can be quite another. Because they have a tremendous amount of power, high-level executives are accustomed to doing and saying whatever they want, making them a unique breed that must be handled with care. Although many managers like to call themselves "executives," only a few really have extensive power, so let's be specific about the people who belong in this category. In the business world, we're talking about the CEO or president of a company—and, if it's a really large organization, possibly their direct reports as well. In the public sector, elected officials and high-level political appointees are really the only ones who qualify. If you are a lowly peon who is fortunate enough—or unfortunate enough, depending on your point of view—to interact with these exalted beings, the following guidelines may help you keep your sanity. And possibly your job.

1. **Don't ever tell executives that they "can't" do anything.** Nothing riles an executive more than being told they can't do something—because you know what? They can if they want to. So saying "you can't" will only start an argument that you will inevitably lose. When you're trying to keep your particular executive from doing something really stupid, try beginning your sentence with, "Yes, we can do that, but let me ask you something . . ." followed by whatever question or concern you may have. Amazingly enough, that simple acknowledgment of their power usually keeps them calm.

2. **Talk fast.** Executives are busy people with tight schedules. They are also very bright people who can absorb information quickly without a lot of explanation. And even if more explanation would be helpful, you're not going to have a chance to give it. Start with your most important points and move quickly, but be prepared for them to pep-

per you with questions after about three sentences. Executives don't want to listen to a monologue. They want to control the conversation, get the information they need, and move on to their next appointment.

3. **Don't expect specific instructions.** Executive brains are usually shifting quickly from one big, important issue to the next, so their instructions are typically about half clear. If you press for specifics, they will become annoyed and decide that you are not too bright. To successfully work with executives, you must possess a certain amount of psychic ability. You must also develop a solid relationship with the person's administrative assistant, who has already learned to read the executive's mind. If you will be working with the executive on a regular basis, the AA is your new best friend.

4. **Make it happen.** Once they have issued some vague directive, executives don't want to hear about that issue again. In their mind, it has been dealt with—by giving it to you—and they have moved on to other matters. They will only return to it if something seems to be going wrong—and you don't want that kind of attention. Avoid going back for more instruction or information. If you can't figure it out yourself, use your networking contacts or pay a visit to the AA.

5. **Take care of the details.** Although you received hazy instructions and are not permitted to return for clarification, you are nevertheless expected to produce a result that is perfect in every respect. Executives hate to deal with details themselves, but they expect flawless execution, assume that all unanticipated obstacles will be overcome, and have absolutely no tolerance for sloppy work. After all, they probably had to meet some pretty tough expectations themselves in order to rise to their lofty position.

6. **Don't take any abuse personally.** Executives can talk to people pretty much any way they want, because, after all, who's going to stop them? That doesn't make it right, of

course. It's just another unfortunate fact of life. If you're forced to deal with an executive who yells, curses, or hurls insults, keep in mind that it's not about you. This is just a high-level person with bad manners. Of course, if the abuse becomes intolerable, you always have the right to stand up for yourself—just recognize that you may be risking your job. When you have the opportunity to exercise power yourself, please do not emulate this childish behavior. Try to be an Adult.

7. **Lose your ego.** Executives were good enough to make it to the top—or very close to the top. They are paid high salaries, given expensive cars, and surrounded with fawning underlings. Hardly anyone ever tells them if they screw up. So executive egos are usually huge, leaving no room for your own little ego problems. If you bring your ego to the party, you'll soon find yourself in a power struggle with an executive—and guess who usually wins those?

8. **Keep your self-confidence.** Ego is not helpful, but self-assurance is a must. Executives despise wimps. They stepped over plenty of those mealymouthed people on their way to the summit. You must therefore master the art of displaying self-confidence while respectfully acknowledging their authority. If you are too deferential or submissive, you will lose all credibility and be viewed as having limited potential.

9. **Hang on to your sense of humor!** You will definitely need it.

Working directly with executives can be a challenge, but anyone with Political Intelligence knows that such exposure provides a tremendous opportunity to expand your influence. And executives are usually bright, savvy people who can be excellent role models and mentors. So put up with their quirks and learn as much as you can. The stress level may be high, but hanging around people who possess immense power is always interesting.

LATERAL INFLUENCE:
COOPERATING WITH CO-WORKERS

Colleagues can be important allies, and making them happy is so, so simple. All you have to do is be consistently agreeable, helpful, and responsive. But because they don't sign our paychecks or write our performance reviews, colleagues often get slighted or overlooked. From a practical standpoint, investing in colleague relationships can return immediate dividends in terms of access to information, contacts with people, and assistance with projects. Looking to the future, you just never know when a co-worker might become your boss—it happens all the time.

1. **Watch for opportunities to help your co-workers.** Share useful information, say something nice about them to management, pitch in when they need an extra hand. If you are a strong, independent type, learn to accept assistance once in a while. People often enjoy feeling helpful.

2. **Return phone calls, answer e-mails, meet deadlines, keep your commitments.** In short, be a reliable, dependable person. Because so many annoying people fail to do these simple things, you can earn a great deal of goodwill by just responding quickly and keeping promises.

3. **Don't expect co-workers to be your therapists.** Recounting the details of your nasty divorce or your traumatic experience with gallbladder surgery usually provides more information than most people want. Unfortunately, they may feel that they have to politely listen until you are through—but if this keeps up, not only will they start to avoid you, they will warn others about you.

4. **Avoid blatant self-promotion, especially at your colleagues' expense.** There is a fine line between appropriately discussing your accomplishments and becoming an annoying braggart. If you habitually feel compelled to display your superior knowledge or top your co-worker's stories, you are probably already known as a showoff. If

you fail to respect boundaries and try to insert yourself into others' projects, they undoubtedly view you as the predator that you probably are.

5. **Be consistently polite and pleasant, even to people who are not.** One of my first bosses had a great attitude about work. "We should be able to do something for everyone who comes into this office," he once said, "even if it's just to give them a pleasant moment in their day." Those wise words have stayed with me ever since. There is absolutely nothing to be gained from offending anyone at work and everything to be gained from being pleasant, even when expressing disagreement.

6. **Discuss concerns with the person involved.** Talking behind someone's back is much easier—and certainly more fun—than facing the person directly. That's probably why the gossiping disease is so widespread. On teamwork surveys, we find that almost every group scores low on coworkers discussing problems directly. But backbiting is the coward's way out, so when you have an issue with someone, screw up your courage and talk about it face-to-face.

7. **When you have difficulties or disagreements, discuss them in an Adult manner.** If you become insulting or critical, you are being a punishing Parent. If you whine or pout, you are acting like a sulky Child. Adults are able to discuss problems, identify shared goals, explore possible solutions, and agree on action steps.

8. **If someone acts rude, impolite, offensive, or insulting, resist the temptation to respond in kind.** Retaliation just brings you down to their level. Maintain an Adult demeanor and eventually they'll calm down. And probably feel pretty stupid. If you experience some quiet satisfaction at this point, that's fine. Just keep it to yourself.

When considering colleagues, you should pay special attention to your **internal customers**—that is, those people who are directly affected by the results you produce. You are particularly important to internal customers, because if *you* do a bad job, *their* work suffers. Some examples: Recruiters find applicants for managers, who are their internal customers. Marketing communication specialists provide advertising materials to the sales force. Intake workers obtain client information that is used by caseworkers. IT specialists keep computer systems running, so virtually everyone is their internal customer. Because they depend on you, internal customers have the potential to become valuable allies or deadly adversaries. To win over your internal customers, communicate with them regularly and solicit their feedback. Ask how you can improve your services and implement any reasonable requests. When you deliver the goods for internal customers, they will praise you to the skies and your reputation will soar. One county tax department threw a surprise party for their IT group to say thanks for their excellent service. On the other hand, if you create difficulties for them, internal customers will quickly spread the word that you are a problem.

DOWNWARD INFLUENCE: THE SECRET OF EFFECTIVE LEADERSHIP

Your company can make you a manager, but your employees decide whether you are a leader. Sadly, many managers fail to see that true leadership has nothing to do with the position they hold. Here's a definition to remember if you want to excel at downward influencing:

A leader is someone that people choose to follow.

Follow, not obey. You can mandate compliance with position power, but only your personal influence will inspire people to go the extra mile and contribute their best efforts. Hundreds of books can provide specific guidance on leadership strategies, but here are some general suggestions for downward influencing.

1. **Realize that you're a manager, not a monarch.** If you really get off on having an important title, a private office, a big desk, a company car, or other symbols of power, get over yourself. You have a bad case of executive-itis (even if you are only a first-line supervisor). Managers with executive-itis feel they should be deferred to by lesser mortals simply because someone put them in a higher position. No one with executive-itis should ever be allowed to become a manager, although they are usually the first to apply for the job. My favorite symptom of this disease is use of the word "insubordinate." Whenever I hear "She's being insubordinate!" I know that we have a manager who is more focused on position power than leadership. A leader is more likely to say, "She really seems upset about something" or "For some reason she isn't following the policy. I need to talk with her about that."

2. **Worry about being respected, not being liked.** Leadership is not a popularity contest. Successful leaders focus on earning respect, not developing friendships. If employees both respect and like you, that's great—but if you're too anxious about their opinions, you'll have trouble making difficult decisions. To have influence, a manager must be able to make the tough calls. So if you have high needs for acceptance, find some fawning friends outside of work. Should this seem to be a persistent and deep-seated problem for you, however, consider whether you really enjoy being a manager. Not everyone does.

3. **Learn to successfully manage the performance of other people.** Managers at all levels must be able to motivate and inspire, set clear goals, give helpful feedback, appreciate good work, implement changes, and address performance issues. They also need to hire the right people and get rid

of those who are never going to get with the program. Unfortunately, however, even long-term executives are often lousy at dealing with performance. No one—let me repeat, *no one*—knows how to do all this without some training. People are usually promoted because they were good at whatever they did before. Then they have to learn how to manage.

4. **Appreciate the power of inclusion.** Learn how and when to involve employees in making decisions, because they know more about the work of your department than you do. If you're a good leader, they will be happy to share their knowledge, and you must also share your knowledge with them. Influential managers know the value of helping employees understand the bigger picture and encouraging them to learn about events beyond their narrow job responsibilities.

5. **Help your employees "be all that they can be."** Insecure managers fear being overshadowed by exceptional people. Leaders want to have as many exceptional people as possible, recognizing that superior performers reflect well on their managers. Some employees simply want to sharpen skills in their current job, while others are motivated by the possibility of doing something more exciting, interesting, or challenging in the future. When you learn about your employees' goals and help them develop in their desired direction, you almost always benefit as well.

Successful managers feel comfortable with power and use it wisely. Those who enjoy dominating others or fear using their authority will never cut it as leaders. Most of us tend to err a little on one side or the other, so learn to recognize your own leadership weaknesses and compensate for them. That's the only way to become an effective manager.

PORTRAIT OF A WINNER

Kate, a human resources manager, provides a great role model for managing power relationships. She has a staff of six, reports to a vice president of administration, and serves on a management team with five other managers. Because of her position, virtually everyone in the company is her internal customer in one way or another. If you were to interview a "full circle" of people who work with Kate, this is how they might describe her.

Pat, VP of Administration: "Kate can work with anybody at any level. I have no reservations about letting her deal directly with the CEO, because I know that she'll use good judgment about what to say and what not to say. She's always respectful, but she'll be the first to tell me if she thinks I'm about to do something stupid—of course, she'd phrase it more diplomatically than that. My other managers tell me that Kate's a good sounding board for them, especially on employee issues. The term 'team player' gets overused, but Kate really is one."

Howard, Finance Manager: "I like working with Kate. The last person in that job was entirely too touchy-feely, had no business sense. But Kate really tries to understand the financial impact of decisions and policies. Not that we always agree—we've been on the opposite side of several issues—but she's willing to listen and compromise. She does a good job of presenting the human side of financial issues. I have to admit that she's changed the way I look at a few things."

Marla, Benefits Specialist: "Kate's my boss, although she's not at all bossy. I wouldn't exactly say she's a friend—I don't know if the person who does your performance review can ever really be your friend—but she's friendly. She's interested in what I'm doing and takes time to listen if I have a problem. When I'm up to my ears in work, she's always willing to pitch in and help. She also lets Pat and the CEO know when we need to make changes to our benefit plans. She's not afraid to speak up to anyone."

Jean, District Sales Manager: "I really don't know Kate all that well, but I've worked with her on a couple of employee problems. We had one sales guy who was making some inappropriate remarks to the secretaries. I don't think his behavior rose to the level of sexual harassment, but it wasn't very professional and someone called HR about it. Kate came out and interviewed the secretaries, then spent some one-on-one time with the sales guy. I'm not sure exactly what kind of magic she worked, but the problem went away. She never lectures like a lot of HR people—she just tries to help."

Kate is a true Winner who builds positive relationships in all directions. Sociopaths, by contrast, focus most of their energy upward. They don't waste much time on peers and employees, because management controls their rewards. Cause-driven Martyrs automatically alienate anyone who appears to be "on the other side" of their chosen crusade—although, ironically, these are usually the very people that they most need to influence. Those Martyrs who wish to please often diminish their political power by spreading themselves too thin, trying unsuccessfully to meet the needs of everyone they encounter. The Dimwits, whose behavior is driven by intense anger or anxiety (or both), will eventually distance themselves from everyone, regardless of power position.

Personal Politics

Do You Have Problems with Power Positions?

Assessing your situation:

- The chart below lists some common problems related to different power positions. Check any with which you identify.

Upward Influence Issues	Lateral Influence Issues	Downward Influence Issues
☐ I tend to get into power struggles and control battles with my boss.	☐ I feel very competitive with my co-workers and always want to be a little better.	☐ I believe that employees should do what their manager tells them to without questioning it.
☐ I resent the fact that my boss has the power to direct my activities.	☐ I tend to avoid working on joint projects or activities with my co-workers and prefer to operate on my own.	☐ I feel that one of the most important tasks of a manager is to point out mistakes and catch errors.

Upward Influence Issues	Lateral Influence Issues	Downward Influence Issues
☐ I sometimes intentionally fail to do something that my boss asks or expects.	☐ I frequently get into arguments with my co-workers.	☐ I sometimes take over my employees' work and wind up doing their tasks.
☐ I tend to feel somewhat anxious when I am with my boss.	☐ I seldom share information with my co-workers.	☐ I feel it is important for my employees to like me as a person.
☐ I am very hesitant about expressing disagreement to my boss.	☐ I am often late meeting schedules and deadlines that affect my co-workers.	☐ I become very uneasy if I feel that employees are unhappy with my decisions or actions.
☐ I often keep my ideas and opinions to myself instead of sharing them with my boss.	☐ I often give co-workers detailed descriptions of my personal problems.	☐ I tend to resent the amount of time that I have to spend dealing with employees' needs and issues.

If you see yourself in any of these descriptions, the odds
are that others see you that way as well. All of these tendencies, beliefs, or actions can create power position
problems.

Moving from assessment to action:

- If you feel that you may have problems with upward, lateral, or downward influence, review the suggestions at
  the end of the appropriate section in this chapter. Set
  some specific goals for changing the way that you relate
  to your boss, colleagues, or employees. You may also wish
  to ask for feedback from people in those positions—just
  be sure not to argue or get defensive if they give you
  some!

Chapter 11

Developing Your
Political Game Plan

When you think about your job, do you get excited or experience a sinking feeling in the pit of your stomach? Does the future look bright or stretch before you like a vast, monotonous wasteland? Are you in control of your destiny or subject to the whims of unpredictable people? For most of us, work consumes at least 50 percent of our waking hours, and that's a lot of time to feel unhappy. To ensure that the occupational part of your life stays on the right track, you should periodically update your Political Game Plan. Depending on your situation, a Political Game Plan can serve several functions:

- Save you from an untimely political suicide
- Help you identify and achieve specific career goals
- Keep you from wasting time and energy on irrelevant distractions
- Provide strategies for dealing with difficult people
- Increase your leverage and build political capital
- Reduce your stress and make your time at work more enjoyable

SIZING UP YOUR POLITICAL SITUATION

The chart below summarizes some fundamental questions to consider in assessing your current political situation. If your answer indicates an immediate problem, the arrow will lead you to a general strategy that is discussed in more detail below. Otherwise, you will simply move to the next question and continue down the path to becoming a political Winner.

The Path to Political Success

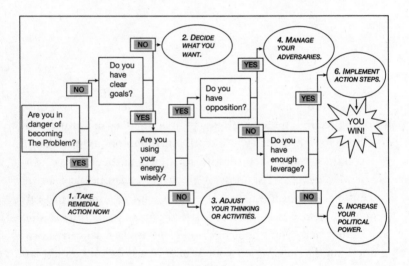

Strategy #1
If you are in danger of becoming The Problem,
then you need to take remedial action immediately.

Should you have the slightest suspicion that you may be viewed as The Problem, pay attention to those feelings. Even if no one has directly mentioned any concerns, your intuition may be picking up some subtle signals. There's no point even thinking about your long-term political objectives until you resolve this immediate issue.

Typically, someone comes to be seen as The Problem for one of three reasons:

1. The person is a Dimwit who wreaks havoc in the workplace by making life more difficult for almost everyone. If you firmly believe that many of your colleagues or managers are obtuse, thoughtless, uncooperative, or difficult to work with, then you might fall into the Dimwit category.

2. The person has become the unfortunate victim of a toxic work environment. In a truly toxic workplace, normal people may be seen as The Problem because they don't conform to the warped standards of a pathological organization. If this reflects your circumstances, then you should relocate to a healthier setting as quickly as possible.

3. The person is acting inappropriately in response to an unwelcome change or a difficult situation. If this sounds like you, then you must rapidly alter your behavior if you want to save yourself. The transformation will probably not be easy, however. If your reputation has deteriorated to the point that you may have been labeled The Problem, then you undoubtedly have some difficult self-management challenges ahead. Your other option, of course, is to take your talents elsewhere.

Extracting yourself from The Problem category and salvaging your career means changing both your feelings and your actions. First, you must get past the "it's not fair" barrier, which can be difficult. Let's make one thing perfectly clear: it does not matter whether or not you have been treated fairly. If the perceived unfairness was so intolerable that you will never get over it, then leave—find another place to work. Staying will only give you an ulcer. If you do stay, and you don't want to be The Problem, then you need to let it go. Shift your focus away from the past and toward the future. When you find yourself mentally reviewing all the gory details of your unjust treatment and seething with resentment, force your thoughts to a calmer place. You must also immediately stop bitching, whining, or complaining to anyone at work. If you have an uncontrollable need to vent, then do so with your spouse, your friend, or your therapist—but tell that person that your goal is to get rid of these feelings. Otherwise they may just join in your pity party and make you even angrier.

Once you have your emotions under control, then you need to formulate a restoration plan. Fairly or not, people have cast you in a negative light, so you must change their perceptions. This may mean taking the initiative to talk with them directly or simply acting differently and waiting for people to notice the "new you." Or, as in the following example, doing both. Wyman, a supervisor, feared that his boss was completely screwing up a highly visible and extremely critical project. He made several attempts to discuss these concerns with his manager, but to no avail. In desperation, he finally sent a written complaint about his boss's mismanagement to the department vice president, with a copy to the human resources manager. Although the resulting series of meetings did help to get the project back on track, Wyman began to sense that he might now be considered a potential Problem. This, of course, seemed quite unfair to him, but lodging a formal complaint about your boss always carries that risk. Wyman managed to keep his feelings about unfairness under control and set about restoring his image. He met with each manager involved to say that he appreciated their listening to his concerns and hoped that everyone could now return to focusing on the project's success. He also made a conscious effort to become extremely helpful, cooperative, and supportive—especially with his boss. In other words, he began acting like the person he wanted them to see.

A restoration plan is designed to give you an image makeover, but you can't expect people to change their opinions overnight. There is always a time lag between behavior change and perception change, so don't get discouraged. If Wyman was previously a pleasant and accommodating fellow, his return to this behavior should allow the memory of his protests to fade fairly quickly. However, if Wyman has been a chronic complainer who now wishes to be viewed differently, the perceptual shift may take longer. Before changing their beliefs, most people have to accumulate evidence over a period of time. The more entrenched the negative image, the greater the amount of evidence needed to erase it. Eventually, though, you will be out of the danger zone and able to focus your energy on more pleasant goals.

Strategy #2
If you are not clear about your goals,
then you need to decide what you want.

Trying to construct a Political Game Plan without a goal in mind is like studying the map before selecting your destination. There's no point plotting the route until you're sure where you want to go. Political strategies that would help you get a promotion may be completely irrelevant if you're planning to start your own business. Consider these fundamental questions about your career goals:

- **Do you want to continue in your current type of work?** If not, what sort of change sounds appealing? If you could wish for any type of job, what would it be? You may want to review the steps that led you to your profession. Did you just take the first position that came along? Did you succumb to pressure from parents, spouse, friends? Or was it a conscious choice based on your interests? Determine whether your career decision was a wise one.

- **Do you want to stay with your current organization?** Is the culture a good "fit" for your temperament and lifestyle preferences? Do you respect the people in leadership positions? Does a meaningful career path exist for you? How does this compare with other places where you have worked? Think about whether you would still like to be there in five years.

- **Do you want to remain in this particular job?** Do you like what you're doing? Is the work challenging enough? Do you enjoy working with your colleagues? Your manager? Are you interested in a promotion? A transfer to another position? Consider how long you are likely to be happy in this role.

If changing your profession, company, or job sounds potentially interesting, then you have a pretty good start on some work-related objectives.

For some people, talking about "goals" can feel kind of intimidating. So if the G-word makes your brain freeze up, just think about what you might like to change, what would be different in your ideal world. One way to generate some ideas is to tap into your creative side by actually drawing a picture of the future, visualizing your perfect life several years down the road. Or if you don't like to draw, just imagine it, then list what you see. Take any part of that picture that relates to work and convert it to a goal. Getting promoted, working in another country, learning a new skill, developing better relationships, earning a degree, having more time for family—all are examples of goals that might show up in a picture of the future.

Strategy #3
If you are not using your energy wisely, then you
need to adjust your thinking or your activities.

During every minute of every day, you are burning mental and physical energy. If you have goals, then a goodly portion of that energy should be directed toward achieving them. Goals automatically provide a useful screening question for your thoughts and actions: "Is this particular use of energy helping to create my desired future?" Sometimes the answer is easy. A few years ago, I was asked to teach an evening MBA course at a local university. Although the role of "professor" had a certain appeal, I quickly discovered that the hours were inconvenient, the pay was meager, and grading papers was a chore. Because my primary goal was to build my consulting practice, not join an academic faculty, the answer to the energy question was obvious. I still teach occasional classes as a guest lecturer, but I'll never be responsible for another course. When two important goals conflict, however, the answer may be more difficult. One of my clients, Tony, is a first-level manager who wants to move up the promotional ladder in a large corporation. He also has a three-year-old son whom he absolutely adores. So when "going the extra mile" at work means coming in on Saturday, how does Tony answer the energy question? It's a tough call, and Tony will probably be juggling those priorities for quite some time.

Sometimes we are thrown off track by internal or external distractions that represent "energy leeches." Try observing yourself for a couple of days with the screening question in mind. See if any of these energy leeches are interfering with your goals.

- **Difficulty focusing:** Do you find yourself bouncing from one task to another with little rhyme or reason? Is your attention easily distracted by anyone who wanders into your office? Do you fall in love with a different idea every week? Multitasking is a useful ability, but when flexibility escalates into being completely scatterbrained, little is accomplished. If this is a challenge for you, then better self-management should become your first priority.
- **Negative emotions:** Some people have a tendency to ruminate endlessly—that is, they obsessively replay past difficulties in their mind, constantly reliving the accompanying unpleasant feelings. Others habitually engage in negative self-talk, focusing on how incompetent, idiotic, or unfair people are. A few hapless souls constantly run the "woe is

me" tape, telling themselves how they can't do anything right, are doomed to fail, and on and on. Regardless of the particular script, all negative feelings drain energy from more productive pursuits; so if you have this problem, you need to begin working on your internal dialogue.

- **Seductive tasks:** Given a choice, we all prefer some tasks and responsibilities over others. But if the stuff you like to do is edging out the stuff you need to do, you may have an energy-use problem, because the stuff you need to do will catch up with you eventually. Put off paying those bills too long and someone will cut off your utilities. You must force yourself to occasionally abandon the fun things and devote sufficient time to the unpleasant but necessary chores required to reach your goals.

- **Toxic people:** Some colleagues add nothing to your life but grief. You may have to work with them, but you have no obligation to eat lunch with them, take breaks with them, listen to their endless complaints, or become their therapist. If this is a problem for you, you're probably being too polite.

Misdirected energy can be a particular hazard for Martyrs. Those who live to please others often sacrifice their own desires in an effort to make other people happy. Because these doormats can easily be taken for granted, their resentment at being underappreciated eventually sucks up even more energy. The other kind of Martyr—those who are obsessed with some cause—often put so much energy into their crusade that important aspects of their work get overlooked. A Martyr's entire personality can easily become one big energy leech.

Strategy #4
If you face opposition in reaching your goals,
then you need to manage your adversaries.

Consider the path between you and your goals. Does anyone seem to be blocking your way? Fuming about your adversary's contrariness or incompetence is just another waste of energy, so politically intelligent people focus on managing their antagonists in an adult manner. If you are currently being thwarted by an adversary, here are some questions to consider.

- **Have you allowed feelings about your adversary to distract you from your goals?** When dealing with an obstructive or difficult person, anger and resentment can hijack your brain and crowd out more productive thoughts and plans. If defeating the adversary becomes your primary goal, then whatever you were originally trying to accomplish is going to get lost.
- **How have you "framed" the situation?** "Framing" is the psychological term for the way we describe our circumstances. The way that you frame a situation usually determines how you act. So if you mentally define the relationship with your adversary as a fight, you are likely to focus your efforts on winning. This thought pattern may cause you to act in a more adversarial manner yourself, thereby escalating the conflict. But if you frame the problem as a difference of opinion or misunderstanding, you are more likely to act in a way that promotes cooperation.
- **Are you sure that the person has evil intentions?** Unless you've developed telepathic abilities, you can't really know another person's motives—you can only make a guess from observing their behavior. If your adversary is belittling your ideas, refusing to share information, failing to meet commitments, or undermining your efforts, it's easy to assume that the person's objective is to see you fail or make your life miserable. But unless you have definite evidence to support this conclusion, cut such people a little slack. They may simply be focused on some goal of their own that has little to do with you personally.

- **Have you considered their point of view?** One way to explore adversaries' possible motivation is to consider various explanations for their antagonistic or annoying behavior. Make an effort to see what the world looks like from inside their "box." What are their most important goals? How is "success" defined in their job? What does management expect from them? What obstacles are they confronting? Are you making their life more difficult in any way? Or blocking the path to their own goals? Try to imagine how they would describe you and your role in this situation.

- **Could the person be "converted" to an ally?** No matter how angry or frustrated you are with your adversary, there's a chance that you might become allies. "No way!" you may be thinking. But consider this: you're running into conflicts because you have to work together, and if you have to work together, then at some level you must have common goals. People with common goals are always potential allies, unless one of them is a Dimwit or a Sociopath. To test this out, you need to engage the other party in a conversation. This may not be an easy or cordial discussion, but if you both have positive intentions, it should be helpful. First, the two of you must agree that you are focused on the future, not the past, and that the goal is problem solving—no blaming or finger-pointing allowed! Then try to follow this agenda: (1) Define your shared objectives; (2) have each person share their point of view while the other listens and does not debate; (3) identify potential strategies for assisting each other; (4) outline steps for a more effective future working relationship. If the other person continues to be hostile, then consider the next two questions. At least you tried.

- **Do you need to increase your leverage?** When you are unable to elicit cooperation from an adversary, then you at least need to prevent the person from impeding your progress. Engaging in a power struggle is seldom a wise move—for one thing, you might lose. However, taking steps to increase your leverage is often the politically intelligent thing to do. First you must calculate the existing leverage equation with this adversary, then figure out how to put more weight on your side.

- **Are other steps needed to "contain" the person?** When collaborative or leverage-building strategies fail to do the trick, then more assertive methods may be needed. Sometimes a direct request to stop disruptive behaviors will succeed where more indirect approaches have failed. Insisting on a clear agreement about job responsibilities, project boundaries, or lines of authority may also be helpful. As a last resort, higher-level managers can be brought in to help resolve the situation, but this tactic should only be used as a desperation measure. Involving higher-ups usually makes them unhappy and may lower their opinion of your ability to solve your own problems. Their participation can also produce all sorts of unintended and undesirable consequences.

We've been considering how to handle a single adversary, but what if you find yourself surrounded by enemies or opponents? If this has happened to you more than once, then you need to take a good, hard look at yourself. There's a fair chance that you're acting like a Sociopath or a Dimwit. If widespread opposition is a new experience for you, however, then you may have landed in an environment that's either completely toxic or just a bad match for your particular work style. In either case, you need to begin a job search, because it's time to move on.

Strategy #5
If you don't have the leverage to get what you want,
then you need to increase your political power.

When you can't achieve a goal on your own, then you are dependent upon other people to make some decisions in your favor. You need sufficient political power to sway their opinions in the desired direction. So who are these people and what could increase your leverage with them? Consider Gina, who feels ready to move into her first management job. For her to be promoted, the right people must believe that she would be a good choice for the next available supervisory slot. These decision-makers might include her current boss, the manager of the open position, higher-level management, and the human resources representative. How does Gina get them to view her as a potential manager? The key to enhancing political power is the Four P's formula that we discussed in chapter 8. See how it may apply to your present situation.

- **Power Assessment:** First, evaluate your current leverage position with critical decision makers. In terms of your immediate goal, what factors are likely to influence them in your direction? Conversely, what could reduce your leverage? In Gina's situation, for example, previous leadership experience would certainly increase her chance of getting a supervisory position, but a highly qualified competitor might interfere.

- **Performance:** In relation to your goal, do you have the knowledge and experience that decision makers view as necessary? What aspects of your work history might be relevant? Would taking on certain responsibilities or tasks increase your leverage? How about attending seminars or workshops? Getting a degree? Gina's leadership credentials would definitely be enhanced by any assignments that require her to head up a committee or lead a project. She might also consider signing up for available workshops on leadership and management.

- **Perception:** How are you viewed by the people who control your desired outcomes? Do they know you? If so, what do they think of your performance? Your attitude? Your desirability as a colleague? What can you do to shape their perceptions? Gina's odds of being promoted will increase if she's viewed positively by upper management. If they've never heard of her, she will seem like more of a risk. And it's a sure bet that she's not getting a management position if she's known as a difficult employee.

- **Partnerships:** Whose help do you need to reach your goal? Are these people already your allies? Or are they adversaries? What could you do to enlist their support? If Gina wants to be a supervisor, a good relationship with her co-workers will be helpful, since management will be wary about promoting anyone who can't get along with colleagues. She may also want to cultivate relationships in the human resources department, which usually has input into promotional decisions.

When trying to boost your leverage, pay special attention to the values and preferences of the Power Elite in your organization, since they will have veto power over almost any decision.

Strategy #6
If you have none of the above political issues,
then you need to move ahead!

This one is easy. You are in good political standing, you know what you want, you're not wasting energy on distractions, you have no obvious opponents, and you have the leverage you need. What's stopping you—Fear? Laziness? Inertia? Well, get moving. List the specific action steps that you need to take, and go for it!

STOP, START, AND CONTINUE

To implement your Political Game Plan you must shift your thinking from strategy to behavior. A simple technique called

"Stop, Start, and Continue" can help you translate global goals into specific steps. The objective of Stop, Start, and Continue is to figure out three things:

1. What are you currently doing that may keep you from reaching your goals? Those are the behaviors or activities you should **Stop**.
2. What new behaviors or activities could help you reach your goals? These are the things you should **Start**.
3. Finally, what are you already doing that is important to achieving your goals? Be sure to **Continue** with those activities.

The answers to these three questions provide the action steps in your Political Game Plan.

Let's illustrate this approach with an example involving two people who work together, but not very successfully. During five years as colleagues, Carolyn and Warren managed to maintain a reasonably civil relationship despite their different work styles. But after Warren was made the manager of the department, some cracks began to appear in this friendly facade. The simmering conflict came to a head when Warren reorganized the unit and assigned Carolyn to a job that she had left two years before. Carolyn promptly lodged a written complaint with Warren's boss, Annette, who had been her manager a few years earlier. In her letter, Carolyn made several scathing remarks about Warren's lack of management ability.

Carolyn's View: "Warren just shouldn't be a manager. He's a nice guy and he means well, but he's totally disorganized. He doesn't plan ahead, doesn't think things through, doesn't communicate . . . and isn't all that what management is supposed to be about? Warren spends a lot of his time fiddling around with our Web site and lets other things—important things—fall by the wayside. Plus, I think he's afraid that I'm after his job, so he never shares any information with me and leaves me completely out of decisions.

Most of the time, I'm the last person to find out anything. That's what this reorganization is really about—getting me out of the way. Warren knows that I'll be totally bored in my old job, so he's hoping I'll just quit. I'm not usually a complainer, but I'm feeling really desperate about this. That's why I sent the letter to Annette. She needs to know how screwed up thing are in this department. I'm afraid she's going to see me as a troublemaker, though."

Warren's View: "Even though she can drive me nuts, I really do believe that Carolyn is a bright, capable person and a valuable employee. But she is obsessive about details and feels she has to know every single thing that's going on in the department. Unexpected changes just seem to throw her off balance. Whenever something doesn't go exactly according to plan, she gets really anxious and keeps coming into my office with one question after another. She just doesn't seem to realize that you can't plan everything in advance. That's why I moved her back into her old position. Things are much more predictable in that job, so I think she'll be more comfortable there. She says that I want her to leave, but that's not true. I'd just like her to calm down! But I do wish she hadn't sent that letter to Annette. Since they used to work together, Carolyn actually knows my boss better than I do. I'm not sure how much credibility I have with Annette at this point."

Annette's View: "I think Carolyn may have a point. Warren is a new manager, and he has a lot to learn. He's very adaptable and flexible, but he's not a natural planner. I've noticed that certain things do seem to be getting a bit out of hand in his department. Although Warren may not realize it himself, I believe he does try to avoid Carolyn. I think she aggravates him. So there may have been a little punishment involved in that reorganization. On the other hand, because I used to be Carolyn's manager, I know that she can be pretty demanding at times. She probably just wears poor Warren out! Carolyn's not comfortable unless she's involved in every decision and understands exactly what's going to happen. She could definitely use a dose of Warren's flexibility. She's a real asset and I don't want her to leave, but I can't let her think that this is some sort of battle that she's 'won.' Warren is Carolyn's boss, and she has to learn how to work with him. I'm going to have a talk with both of them. I really hate this kind of thing!"

Like many workplace dramas, this one doesn't have any heroes or villains—just two people who are trying to do a good job in their very different ways. To demonstrate Political Intelligence, they each need to start giving some thought to the future. Unless some changes are made, Carolyn is in danger of becoming The Problem, and Warren risks failing in his first management job. Learning to cooperate will benefit both of them. This is what a useful Political Game Plan might look like for Warren and Carolyn:

Warren's Political Game Plans

Stop	*Start*	*Continue*
• Leaving employees out of decisions that affect them • Avoiding Carolyn when she wants to talk to me • Spending so much time working on the Web site	• Devoting more time to planning • Setting aside a regular weekly time to meet with each employee • Reassessing Carolyn's current job assignment • Looking for an appropriate management workshop to attend • Delegating Web site work to employees	• Meeting with Annette weekly to update her on department activities

Carolyn's Political Game Plans

Stop	Start	Continue
• Rushing into Warren's office whenever I think of a question • Complaining to my colleagues about Warren • Complaining to Annette about anything	• Trying to be more relaxed about changes at work • Meeting with Warren at regular times • Talking with Warren about the kind of work I would like to do • Doing less talking and more listening	• Doing the best job I can in the position that I currently have, even if it's boring

To join the Winners' club, you have to adopt certain attitudes and behaviors that consistently demonstrate Political Intelligence. Having a specific road map to follow greatly increases your odds of solving political problems and reaching important goals. When you focus on the specific things that you yourself can do differently, and stop wasting time wishing that others would change, you increase your political power and put yourself in charge of your own destiny.

Personal Politics

What Is Your Political Game Plan?

Assessing your situation:

- As you follow the flow chart and review the political strategies, which seem most applicable to your situation? What do you need to do to begin implementing that strategy?

Moving from assessment to action:

- To turn general strategies into a Political Game Plan, create your own Stop, Start, and Continue list as shown below. Instead of listing generalities like "communicate better," be sure to state specific behaviors, like "pay more attention when my colleagues are telling me about their projects."

Your Political Game Plan

Stop	*Start*	*Continue*

- Review your Stop, Start, and Continue list on a regular basis and grade yourself on your progress. As you achieve your goals or the situation changes, revise your game plan and update your list.

Chapter 12

A Personal Political Note

Most of our traits are the product of nature, nurture, and learning—and Political Intelligence is no exception. Looking back, I can recall two specific moments when I recognized that I possessed certain innate abilities that were politically useful. The first occurred when I was district manager of a state government office in Chapel Hill, North Carolina. Sitting at my desk one day, pondering how to get some new policy or program approved by our central office, I realized that the path to success was quite clear: who should be included in the decision, what information they needed to have, the order in which I should talk to these people, and so forth. At that instant, it occurred to me that I apparently had a knack for navigating this type of situation. Fully developed interpersonal road maps would just pop into my head whenever I needed to get something accomplished.

The second event happened some years later in the small conference room of a large technology company in Atlanta. As human resources director, I was attending a meeting led by one of our senior vice presidents. Listening to him rant about some business issue, I remember being amazed that he would make his own insecurities and worries so obvious in such a public setting. After the meeting, when I shared my observations with a couple of colleagues, they looked at me blankly and said that he seemed fine to them. Two days later, the announcement came that this senior VP was leaving the company "to pursue other opportunities"— business language for "he's being fired." This episode made me realize that not everyone has an antenna that picks up emotional signals.

My parents probably provided me with a political head start in life, although they never would have thought of it that way. My dad, a government executive, was a master at navigating political minefields. And my mother, whose work always involved helping others, was a brilliant people-reader. Even more important were the values that they demonstrated in their daily lives and instilled in their children. I offer these basic beliefs not only as a set of wise rules to live by, but also as a summary of political fundamentals.

1. **Be honest and ethical in all your dealings with people.** When everyone lived in small towns and did business only with their neighbors, a dishonest merchant or trades-man quickly acquired a bad reputation and lost business. These days, it may take a little longer for the word to spread, but the result will eventually be the same. If people find they can't trust you, you will lose credibility.

2. **Believe in yourself.** If you don't, why should anyone else? Insecure people usually compensate for their self-doubt in politically destructive ways. If you lack confidence, find a friend, mentor, or therapist who can help you discover your strengths. As a parent, remember that self-confidence is one of the greatest gifts that you can give your children.

3. **Believe in your work.** Much of your time on this planet will be spent doing various jobs. If you can find a sense of purpose in these activities, you will be a happier and more effective person. Performing meaningful work doesn't require you to emulate the saints or discover a cure for

cancer. Every single occupation makes a contribution to society—you simply need to find one that you personally feel good about.

4. **Do the best job you can.** If you are a high achiever, you may be surprised to learn that most people are not. Only a rather small percentage of folks really give their all at work. But these self-starters are greatly appreciated by those who hand out the corporate goodies, because they can always be counted on to deliver results.

5. **Keep your commitments.** If you would like surefire strategy for blowing your career, become undependable. Miss deadlines, screw up schedules, neglect to provide information, forget to submit reports, fail to return phone calls. One of the nicest work compliments you can receive is to be told that people can always count on you.

6. **Be a pleasant person.** People aren't too different from lab rats: we seek out rewarding experiences and steer clear of punishing ones. If interaction with you is a disagreeable event, people will avoid it. Sustaining a successful career is tough when no one wants to talk with you.

7. **Feel true respect for everyone.** The operative word here is "feel." You can act polite and respectful, but if you don't believe that someone truly has worth, they will know. Perhaps the most important message that my brother and I received growing up was that everyone has value. Money, status, position, titles—none of that mattered. What did matter was the way someone lived their life and treated other people.

When I think about the relatively small number of people that I would classify as unconditional, genuine, 100-percent Winners, they all seem to share these beliefs. So I highly recommend these qualities to you.

In addition to being excellent role models, my parents made one other contribution to my political education. Although they shared similar values, the two people who brought me into this world had very, very different personalities and temperaments. As a tot, I expect that my tiny brain was constantly puzzled by the dissimilar expectations and habits of my quiet, reserved, analytical, organized father and my outgoing, spontaneous, emotional, creative mother. But they provided terrific training in learning to deal with different types of people, one of the most useful political skills. Which may be why my brother and I can get along amiably with just about anyone! For me, this learning has been reinforced by my experiences in nonprofit, government, and business organizations. Different missions, different cultures, and very different kinds of folks. Exposure to a variety of people and places will broaden your political horizons.

Early experiences are important, but Political Intelligence is also a learned ability. Despite my helpful upbringing, I was a political idiot in my first professional job, where I managed to make an enemy of my boss's wife, with whom I shared an office. (Yes, it was a pretty weird situation, but I could have handled it better.) After years of learning—from events, mentors, books, workshops, and life in general—I have more political street smarts now. This book was written in the hope of shortening that learning process for others by openly discussing some fundamental political realities. Most people, I believe, want to spend their days doing meaningful work in a friendly, collaborative environment. Yet I continually encounter bright, talented, well-intentioned folks who have gotten themselves into some sort of stressful and frustrating political muddle. When they are able to shift their thinking patterns or adopt different behaviors, the situation often improves.

One of my favorite sayings, by Joseph Addison (1672–1719), is this: "The great essentials of happiness are something to do, something to love, and something to hope for." Work is a large part of that equation. And politics are an inescapable aspect of work. So I wish you the best of luck with your political challenges and hope that you are able to achieve the goals that matter to you, whatever they may be.

Suggested Reading

Arbinger Institute, The. *Leadership & Self-Deception*. San Francisco: Berrett-Koehler, 2002.

Badaracco, Joseph. *Leading Quietly*. Boston: Harvard Business School Press, 2002.

Covey, Stephen. *The Seven Habits of Highly Effective People*. New York: Free Press, 2004.

Finkelstein, Sydney. *Why Smart Executives Fail*. New York: Penguin Group, Inc., 2004.

Goleman, Daniel. *Emotional Intelligence*. New York: Random House, 1997.

McGinty, Sarah. *Power Talk: Using Language to Build Authority and Influence*. New York: Warner Business Books, 2002.

Tannen, Deborah. *Talking from 9 to 5*. New York: HarperCollins, 1995.

Waldroop, James, and Timothy Butler. *The 12 Bad Habits That Hold Good People Back*. New York: Random House, 2001.

Index

About the Author

Marie G. McIntyre, Ph.D., operates Executive Counselors, a training and consulting business focused on developing leadership and teamwork in organizations. She has more than twenty years of experience in management, organizational development, and training. Dr. McIntyre works with business, government, and nonprofit organizations, including such clients as The Home Depot, Prudential Financial, BellSouth, and Panasonic. In addition to holding management positions in both business and government, she was director of human resources for a Fortune 500 company. Dr. McIntyre, who also wrote *The Management Team Handbook,* lives in Atlanta, Georgia.